# Mistaken
*for a* King

ALSO BY DAN KELLAMS

*A Coach's Life: Les Hipple and the Marion Indians*

# Mistaken
## *for a* King

### *Sketches of a*
### *Small-Town Boyhood*

*To Jim & Sylvia —*

*Dear Classmates + friends*

*Dan Kellams*

*7-29-16*

# Dan Kellams

PUBLISHING

Mistaken for a King
Sketches of a Small-Town Boyhood

Portions of this book appeared in a different form
in the *Wapsipinicon Almanac, MetroSportsReport.com,*
and the *Litchfield* (Connecticut) *County Times*

Cover and interior design by Kari Johnston.
Main Street mosaic by Karen Hoyt,
courtesy of the Marion Heritage Center.

ISBN 978-0-692-72976-2

FAIT Accompli Publishing
Phoenix, Arizona
602-466-8128

*For Stanley, Margaret, and Pete*

*And for Elaine*

*What are all these fragments for,*
*if not to knit up finally?*

– Marilynne Robinson


*Life passes into pages*
*if it passes into anything.*

– James Salter

# CONTENTS

## *Author's Note: Predicament on a Roof*

JEAN RENOIR, the great French film director, is credited with saying, "The only things that are important in life are the things you remember."

I remember three boys sitting in a row on the roof of a garage, their knees pulled up under their chins, their arms wrapped around their legs. They aren't supposed to be up there.

I am one of the boys. My best friend, Tom, is another. I'm not sure who the other is. I'm pretty sure it's not my younger brother, Pete.

The garage is next to the house my parents built a few years earlier. We have ascended to the roof by putting a ladder against a tree next to the garage, climbing the ladder to a notch in the tree, scaling the tree up to a branch that hung out over the garage, then edging out on the branch to attain the roof. It was not as easy as we thought it would be.

We wanted to make a quick scramble to the roof and then jump off before anyone caught us.

But from up here the distance to the ground looks much farther than it did when we were down there. Besides, the landing area is not good. The ground slants downhill, from our right to left, and it is lined with flagstones that make steps down the hill. It is a hard, uneven place to complete a ten-foot leap. We had not properly anticipated that.

The reason I'm pretty sure the third boy was not my little brother is that I would have made him jump off to test the descent. If Pete were injured, the survivors could prudently climb back down. If he landed unhurt, we still had options.

Now, here's the thing. This happened decades ago. I can't remember what we did. A guy can't remember everything, and the rules I set for myself in writing this book don't allow me to make things up—certainly not events as major as jumping off a garage. There are things you remember, and, if you dwell on them for a while, they will lead to things you imagine you remember. I have tried to stick with the former and avoid the latter.

So I can't make up a story for you. We were up there, that's all.

A characteristic of old memories is that they are episodic; brief flashes of light—clearly illuminated scenes and events—surrounded by darkness. A scene from a movie, projected against the night sky, vivid but unfinished and unconnected. Or a pencil sketch rather than a fully conceived painting. This then is a book of sketches dictated by strong memories and grouped by subject matter, not chronology, roving backward and forward through a few glorious years in the life of a boy. Feel free to read them in any order that suits you.

This is how we lived then, in a small Iowa town in the middle of the last century.

# I.

## MARGARET AND STANLEY

## A Love Story

MARGARET HARTUNG was born January 14, 1907, and grew up in Mount Vernon, Iowa. Stanley Kellams was born April 10, 1907, and grew up in Marion, Iowa. The two towns are about fifteen miles apart in eastern Iowa. Margaret and Stanley met at Cornell College in Mount Vernon. This probably happened in the fall of 1927. No one knows how or when their romance began.

Margaret's father was a banker in Mount Vernon. The family seemed well-to-do, occupying a large Victorian house on an oversized lot. But Margaret's father contracted tuberculosis in middle age. Margaret said years later that her dominant memories of living in that house were the demands by her mother that she remain quiet while her father rested in his room upstairs—and the sounds of him wheezing and coughing. Despite the relative grandeur of the house, money was tight. When Cornell College was in session, the Hartungs rented their upstairs sleeping porch to students.

Margaret was the middle child, bracketed by two brothers. All three went to Cornell College and became educators. The oldest was Maurice (pronounced

Morris), who became a professor at the University of Chicago and wrote several widely used college mathematics textbooks. Margaret's younger brother, Francis, became a high school administrator. Margaret became a teacher.

A photo of Margaret probably taken during her twenties shows her to be what might be called "handsome." She was not a beauty, but neither plain. Her dark hair is cut short, in a wavy bob, quite in style for the 1920s. She would wear her hair short for the rest of her life, for the convenience of it, perhaps. She had brown eyes. She stood about five feet three, heavy-boned but not fat. She came from a stoical, frugal, hardworking family, and she demonstrated those characteristics throughout her life. She was intelligent and could be critical of others, not always silently.

Stanley was the younger of two brothers. Their mother was a tiny, feisty woman who enjoyed a good joke. Their father, who was nearly six feet tall, was variously a telegraph operator, a railroad mail clerk, a failed insurance salesman, and a successful restaurant operator.

According to the scant evidence that survives, Stanley and his older brother, Lester, lived the barefoot life typical of small-town boys of the time, fishing and swimming in the creek, playing ball in the fields, working at whatever jobs became available. For a time when they were in grade school, the boys took a little girl to class with them. She was too young for school, three or four, but she went along with them and sat quietly while the older children attended to their lessons. It was as if the boys had brought a patient dog into the classroom. When school ended, or perhaps during lunch hour, the boys took the little girl home.

Lester and Stanley went to Marion High School where they were both first-string athletes. Lester, two years older than Stanley, was quarterback on the football team and guard in basketball. Stanley twice led his basketball teams in scoring despite the fact that he could not straighten his left arm, which had been broken and did not heal properly.

Stanley stood about five feet nine inches. He had a narrow face with protruding ears, and he began to go bald at an early age. He was anything but handsome, yet he possessed a crooked smile, gentle sincerity, a sly wit, and an open nature that girls found attractive. He had blue eyes.

At Cornell College, Margaret was two classes ahead of Stanley. He had delayed his entrance after high school to work on a pea farm in Illinois, probably to raise money for college. During this period, Stanley visited Chicago. One night as he stood innocently nearby, he saw a man killed by a shotgun blast in an alley. Stanley did not care much for big cities.

Margaret and Stanley never told their sons the story of how they met and how their romance developed, perhaps because they were never asked. After graduating from college in 1928, Margaret chose one of the few career paths that welcomed women. She found a position teaching English in Odebolt, a village in western Iowa, where she became principal of the junior high school.

Stanley dropped out of college after three years and joined his father and mother working in the K-V Café in Marion, which his father had established in 1931.

Odebolt, where Margaret worked, was two hundred miles from Marion, where Stanley lived. That was a very long way. Roads were poor, cars unreliable, and Iowa was deep in an economic depression. It is not certain that Stanley owned a car. Perhaps Margaret returned to Mount Vernon in the summer, when school was out, and they saw each other then. Perhaps Stanley made trips to Odebolt by train or bus when he could. Long distance phone calls were expensive and generally reserved for emergencies. They probably wrote a lot of letters.

In 1934, they considered marriage. Margaret had now worked six years as a teacher; she was twenty-seven years old. Most women were married before they reached that age. She faced a crucial decision. She could marry Stanley or she could continue teaching, but she could not do both. Public schools, even colleges, terminated female teachers if they married. There were two reasons for this: One is that school officials believed that married women did not need a job because they had husbands to provide for them. It would thus be a greater social good during hard times to employ an unmarried woman, who had no means of support, or a young husband, who had a wife to look after. The other reason for not allowing young married women to continue as teachers was that they soon became pregnant. This condition was deemed unsuitable for the classroom—and, besides, the woman would leave the workforce when her baby arrived.

So Margaret stood at a crossroads. She could continue her professional career or she could be married and have children. There were no two ways about it.

Stanley also thought seriously about marriage. When I was a young boy, prying into boxes and trunks in the attic of our house, I found a letter Stanley had written to Margaret before their wedding. The letter did not gush with passion; he did not praise her eyes, her mouth, her touch. There may have been letters like that, but I found only one, the one Margaret saved. In it, Stanley raised hard questions about the future. Concern about financial survival was only one topic. Stanley also wrote—and as I remember it, he did so in a series of questions—about what marriage would require of them: cooperation, tolerance, and dedication to mutual goals. Were they, he asked Margaret, truly ready and willing to fulfill those requirements for the rest of their lives, to make the personal sacrifices that marriage required? Were they prepared to subdue their egos and put the needs of their relationship ahead of their desires as individuals? Although I was very young when I found that letter, it impressed me with its gravity and honesty. I felt embarrassed and put it back without reading it all.

Margaret said yes. They were married on the last day of school in 1934 in Ida Grove by the Ida County justice of the peace. Stanley bought a new Arrow shirt and borrowed a car from Margaret's brother Francis. No relatives attended the wedding; two teachers from Odebolt served as witnesses. It was a typical Depression-era wedding, simple and inexpensive. There was no honeymoon. The couple drove back to Marion, where they were to live with Stanley's parents and work with them at the K-V Café.

Stanley's father, Roy, had given up trying to sell insurance in 1931 and started the K-V Café on a Marion side street. In 1934, the restaurant moved to Main Street, occupying a building that had previously been an A&P grocery. Here it became what was probably the leading restaurant in town. Light poured in through a large plate-glass window. Booths ran along the east wall, a few tables occupied the center of the room, and a row of stools lined a counter near the west wall behind the cashier's station. Local merchants came in daily for coffee and conversation. A room behind the kitchen was available for private parties. The Lion's Club and other groups met there. High school kids came in and danced to the music of a jukebox in the back room.

The initials *K* and *V*, we were told, stood for Kellams and Vernon. Pete and I never knew who Vernon was or what role he played in the enterprise.

Back in Marion, Margaret and Stanley had a room with Stanley's parents, jobs in the restaurant, and free meals there. They were fortunate. It was the time of the Great Depression. Millions were out of work, homeless, and hungry. Stanley worked as a cook. Margaret waited tables. He was paid one dollar a day; she received twenty-five cents. Stanley's father, Roy, paid them every day because he was never certain of the next day's cash flow. Although Roy's wife, Cleora, was cheerful and energetic, Margaret felt oppressed in the same home as her mother-in-law.

The couple's first child, a son, was born August 25, 1936, during a prolonged heat wave. The hospital bill was preserved in a baby book. The operating room fee was $7.50; surgical dressings cost $3.50; medicines $2.75. As was the custom, Margaret stayed in the hospital a long time—eleven days. Room, board, and general nursing costs came to an even $55.

A second son was born February 20, 1939. By this time, the couple had secured an apartment and adopted a dog, a pug named Simon, and Margaret was now a housewife. It was not a role she would play exclusively for long.

It should perhaps be said here, although there will be sufficient evidence later, that Margaret and Stanley lived up to the standards suggested in the prenuptial letter. Their sons have no memory of them fighting or even raising their voices against one another. Surely they had disagreements, but they somehow settled them out of their children's hearing. In dealing with their sons' desires, needs, and rebellions, they were a united front.

Sometimes, on a road trip, tension arose between Margaret and Stanley over the selection of a restaurant or motel. Margaret usually prevailed. Stanley rarely used profanity, and then only when he was very angry, having to shout out a hell or damn to quiet his sons who were squabbling in the back seat of the car. Margaret never swore. On road trips, Stanley kept the car radio turned off; he wanted to focus on driving safely.

The most off-color joke Stanley told, and he did not tell it until his children were in high school, went like this: Eat every bean and pea on your plate. Your mother doesn't like to wash dishes.

Margaret and Stanley did not drink alcohol when they were raising their children. They drank black coffee and smoked cigarettes. Stanley smoked Camels, blunt little cigarettes before the advent of filters. Sometimes, to save money, he rolled his own cigarettes using a small plastic device to bind the tobacco in a sheet of paper. He lit his cigarettes with a steel Zippo lighter, which he could bring to flame with two snaps of his fingers, the first to fling open the lid, the second to send sparks flying from the flint into the wick.

Margaret, always careful with money, smoked Wings, an economy brand. She lit them with kitchen matches, pulled from a box she used to light the oven.

Wings not only were longer than most cigarettes but also cost less, so by smoking them Margaret was saving two ways. A third benefit of Wings was that they came packed with little cards bearing photos of airplanes. In her time as a teacher Margaret almost certainly was forbidden from smoking in public. She maintained the practice after she married, seldom smoking outside her home or those of friends, and never on the street.

Margaret did not drive a car. The reason is unknown. She walked uptown to Marion to shop or took a bus to downtown Cedar Rapids, only a few miles away. Or Stanley drove her. Margaret managed the money. Stanley handled disciplinary issues with the children, which rarely involved spanking. He was a tolerant parent, which his sons appreciated. The remorse they felt when they disappointed him was often punishment enough. Although Stanley had been a restaurant cook, Margaret prepared all the meals. When it came to dishes, she washed, he wiped. On Saturdays, when they cleaned house together, he always did the vacuuming.

In a multitude of ways Margaret and Stanley bent their lives to serve the interests of their sons. They made a gift of themselves.

THESE ARE my memories of the years my parents worked at the K-V Café and we lived in an apartment in the south of town.

I am very shy. When my mother introduces me to adults, I cannot answer their questions. I put my head down and press closer to her leg, holding her dress. I am speechless.

One day I decide to pretend I am not shy. The lady asks me a question, and I answer it brightly, with a shake of my head. The lady laughs in delight, and I smile a little. I realize that if I pretend I am not shy, people will not know I am shy. But I am still shy, just not so much.

MY PARENTS want to go on vacation. I am three years old. Grandma Kellams will take care of my baby brother, and I am to stay with Grandma Hartung in Mount Vernon. I don't want to. I don't want to be away from my parents. I don't like Grandma Hartung. She never has candy when we visit.

My parents drive me to Mount Vernon and lead me up the big steps to the front porch. Grandma Hartung comes out and holds me by the shoulder as we say goodbye to my mother and father. I begin to cry. As they drive off I start screaming. I struggle against her grasp and scream.

My parents drive around the block, see me shrieking on the porch as Grandma Hartung grips my shoulders with both hands. They decide to cancel their vacation. In the car as we drive toward home I stop crying.

I AM four years old. Some misbehavior of mine, some mischief I repeat often, upsets my mother. She tells me that if I continue to do it, she will leave me; she will run away. I don't believe her. I continue in this behavior—perhaps it involves tormenting my little brother—but she does not leave. Mothers can't leave.

Then one day, she leaves. She walks out the door, goes down the sidewalk, crosses the street, and enters a house. I watch her do this from a window. She has disappeared.

I am terrified and begin crying. My little brother, too young to understand what is happening, senses my panic and begins to cry as well. In some way, for the first time, I realize that I am helpless.

Then the door across the street opens, my mother comes out, calmly crosses the street, and comes back home.

WE ARE at the K-V Café. It is mealtime for the employees. My mother sits at the counter with other workers, eating supper. I stand nearby, just behind her.

As Margaret finishes her meal she asks for a second helping of mashed potatoes. She is told—by my grandfather, perhaps—that she may have more potatoes or she may have ice cream for dessert. She has to choose one or the other.

My mother opts for the potatoes. I am amazed that she should make such a choice. I would never have passed up ice cream for potatoes.

It does not occur to me to wonder why she couldn't have both.

I AM tempted daily by the assortment of candies at the cashier's stand at the K-V Café. The candies cost a few pennies: foil-wrapped chocolates, hard candies, soft white mints with a green, jelly-like filling. I especially covet Peanut Butter Logs, which lie in a small pile on a green-tinted, transparent glass plate. The plate is shaped like a leaf.

Peanut Butter Logs are a few inches long, smaller than a candy bar, larger than a mint. They are striped in cream and brown. They are sealed in cellophane and cost a penny, or perhaps two cents. I have no money and when I ask my parents to buy me a Peanut Butter Log they usually say no.

I think about biting into a Peanut Butter Log. It is crunchy on the outside—the hard coating shatters sweetly against the tongue—and softer in the middle. It tastes like peanut butter and sugar.

I sometimes stand near the cashier's desk and look at the candy. I survey the number of Peanut Butter Logs on their green plate. Would one be missed? I know it is wrong to take candy without paying. Then one day when no one is looking I steal a Peanut Butter Log and stuff it in my pocket.

Later, alone, I eat it. My mouth is dry and the little bar tastes like dust. I sense that my parents know of my theft. They know I betrayed them. I steal no more candy.

# II.

# AROUND THE HOUSE

## *The Homestead*

IN THE summer of 1941, with war raging in Europe and Asia, Stanley and Margaret purchased a vacant lot on north Eighteenth Street in Marion, Iowa. It was one of the last undeveloped lots on the street. Pastures and farmland lay behind it. The lot measured eighty-six by one hundred twenty feet. On it, the couple built a small, two-bedroom bungalow with an unfinished basement, an unfinished attic, and an unattached one-car garage. The total cost for land and buildings was $4,500. They had been married for seven years and had two sons. I turned five that summer; my little brother, Pete, was two and a half.

We lived there nine years.

Considering their meager wages at the K-V Café, it's hard to imagine how Stanley and Margaret were able to make the down payment and secure a loan on an investment of this magnitude. But Margaret was frugal, and probably had saved a portion of her salary during her six years as a teacher. Her mother may have been able to lend the couple some money; it is unlikely that Stanley's parents had any to spare. In a year or two, Stanley would find an office job with a manufacturer of earth-moving equipment in Cedar Rapids, and this surely helped the family's income.

My parents must have felt lucky. They had survived the Depression and realized the American dream of home ownership, and they had done so just in time—housing construction came to a virtual halt after America entered World War II in December of that year, just a few weeks after we moved into the house.

The footprint of the house was less than one thousand square feet. Inside were four small rooms. The living room contained a few chairs and a sofa, above which hung a picture of a schooner at full sail on white-capped seas. On the south wall was a small bookcase holding offerings from the Book of the Month Club and *Reader's Digest* condensed books. Next to the bookcase, French doors led to a small screened porch. A drop-leaf dining table sat against the north wall. We passed it on the way to the front door but rarely ate there.

The kitchen held a small wooden table with just room for four, and we took all our meals there. The table was painted a light green, suggesting it was old and had been refinished. A small radio sat on the table. On Sunday evenings, for supper, Margaret made sandwiches and popped enormous mounds of white popcorn. She purchased the corn from a local farmer named Lyle Touro, who made the rounds selling his produce by the sack. It was available shelled or on the cob. Margaret bought it shelled and poured the kernels into a film of oil in a skillet. As the corn began to pop she shook the skillet to keep the kernels evenly distributed. The aroma was heavenly. Then she dumped the popped corn into a white enameled basin large enough to soak one's feet.

As we shoveled down the popcorn and Margaret refilled the basin, we listened to the Sunday night comedy lineup on the radio. First came Fred Allen, whose biting witticisms often went over my head. In another program, Jack Benny's gentle self-mockery about his age, stinginess, and poor violin playing always made me giggle. So did Edgar Bergen and Charlie McCarthy, the former a ventriloquist, the latter a dummy, but a very sharp-tongued one who, we knew from the movies, wore a top hat, white tie, and monocle. Charlie exchanged insults with comedian W.C. Fields and flirted with the glamorous Dorothy Lamour. I was especially fond of Mortimer Snerd, a wonderfully simple-minded dummy whose stupidity seemed very funny at the time but might be considered offensive today.

There were two bedrooms in the house. The one belonging to our parents was basically off limits. My brother and I shared the other, which contained two single beds covered with blue spreads dotted by white sailboats, curled ropes, and other seafaring motifs. For a time the beds were stacked as bunks, but as my brother grew older, there were disputes over which of us should get the top bunk. If my brother was in the top bunk, I often lay below him, kicking up with my feet so hard he almost bounced to the ceiling. This took the form of cooperative rough play or downright bullying, depending on our moods. Our parents addressed the problem by dismantling the beds and separating them with a small desk.

There was one bathroom, a sink, toilet, and tub, between the two bedrooms. The telephone was also in this hallway. It was made of hard black plastic and had no dial. To use it, which we did rarely, we picked up the handset and waited for the operator to come on.

She said, Number please, and we gave her one, such as 424 or 367-J, and she put the connection through. Conversations were brief and businesslike. A phone was not meant for idle chatter. Pete and I typically sought permission before using it.

When Pete and I were small we occasionally were allowed to roughhouse in the living room. One evening, not long after we moved in, we played a game as our parents sat nearby, laughing. I held Pete by one arm and one leg and swung him in a circle. Pete and I were laughing too—and eating peanuts. Suddenly Pete choked and began gasping for air. A peanut had lodged in his windpipe. He was rushed to the hospital, where he spent several days. Our mother stayed with him. One day she came home to handle some matters. She told me this story several times. I knew she was coming and ran up to the top of the hill to meet her and said, I want you to come home right now. There is no record that I inquired about Pete's condition.

The house was not large enough to absorb our energy. There was no television to sedate us. We were still quite young when our parents adopted the only reasonable response to the pandemonium we caused in the house. Stanley ordered us, If you are going to keep doing that, go outside or down to the basement. The basement held an oil furnace and our mother's washing machine, a green wringer-washer. The clothing was washed and rinsed in an agitating bin, then fed through a wringer by hand before being hung on a clothesline to dry. There wasn't much to do down there. If it wasn't raining, we usually went outside.

OUR HOUSE was near the top of a hill, and the land fell away from it in two directions: sharply downhill to the north and more gently to the east, giving the backyard a slight slope from the house to the back property line.

The garage had been neatly fitted between two trees, an apple tree on the north side, good for climbing but essentially barren of fruit. A larger tree sat close to the garage on the south side, its branches reaching over the garage roof. It would require a ladder to scale the first six feet or so, but after that the tree offered a route to the top of the garage, and it became one of our goals to work our way up there and then jump off.

On the north side of the garage, where our property abutted our neighbor's, a tall stand of shrubbery formed an arch over a barren spot of earth. The area between the shrubs created an arbor just large enough for two of us to crawl in and find shelter. We played there sometimes, in this small, cave-like opening. Whenever we heard stories or read books about secret passageways or hidden gardens, we knew what they looked like, because we had one too.

A small garden sat in the far northeastern corner of our lot. It featured a grape trellis that mysteriously seemed to pre-date our arrival. With great reluctance in the best of years the vines bore a few globes of fruit, tough skinned and sour. We believed the grapes were bad for our stomachs, and left them for the birds, whose purple droppings dotted the driveway. Our parents tried to plant a Victory Garden there; the government encouraged citizens to grow their own vegetables, thus leaving more food for the war effort. The garden did not flourish.

To the south, a towering wall of closely planted shrubbery screened the house uphill from ours. This dense planting was a clear signal that the occupants wanted privacy. Even the front of the house was shielded by bushes and trees. Our father warned us, more than once, to stay out of this neighbor's property. The owners did not welcome children.

However, temptation in the form of a small, white, concrete-lined fish pond lay at the very back corner of their lot, barely visible to us from our side of the shrubs. As we crawled to the edge of the shrubbery, we could glimpse fish swimming in the pond. *Real fish! Right next door!* We could not resist. Doing our best to become invisible, my best friend, Tom, Pete, and I squirmed through the undergrowth and crawled to the pond. There, hunched over, we watched the orange fish patrol their watery prison. We noted their reaction to such stimuli as sticks and leaves. We scratched the earth, but could find no worms or bugs for them. Satisfied, we crawled back to safety.

Later that day, our father told us we were never to go into the neighbor's yard again. To do so would result in severe punishment. He really meant it, and we contented ourselves thereafter by crawling to the edge of the bushes and peering from our side at what little we could see of the fish. Before long, the fish disappeared and the little pool went dry.

The eastern limits of our backyard were marked by a row of tall bushes. An alleyway lay just beyond that. The alley was little used, unpaved, overgrown with grass. Beyond the alley was a large garden maintained by a neighbor who also kept a cow and some chickens. The garden gave way to pastures, a small stream, and a few stands of trees. Beyond that, farther than we needed or wanted to go, cornfields stretched for miles. We awoke in the morning to roosters crowing.

## *Spike, Donald, and a Cat*

IN THOSE days, in farm country, it was common for children to acquire animals from well-meaning adults who gave them baby chicks or rabbits to mark holidays, thinking, perhaps, that caring for the little creatures might teach the children responsibility. Baby chicks dyed in Easter pastels were easily purchased. We kept them in a crudely fenced pen behind the garage. We did not think of them as pets. Perhaps Pete and I fed them; perhaps our mother did. Few survived to adulthood, at which point they disappeared, sold off or given away by our parents.

A white duck named Donald was an exception. Something about his ducky strangeness appealed to my brother and me, and so he stayed with us longer than the others. It was our hope to make friends with him, but Donald wasn't interested. A ball of yellow feathers when we adopted him, Donald grew into a cranky adult. There was neither recognition nor gratitude in his agate-like stare when we offered him, through the fence, a morsel of bread. Instead of gently taking the food, he snapped at our fingers.

Donald was a Houdini among ducks. One day he

escaped his pen and set off in search of a better life, presumably one that included a body of water. When we found him gone, we mounted a rescue operation, my father at the wheel of his Chevrolet. Perhaps concerned about what the neighbors might think, Stanley was relentless in his effort to capture Donald and bring him home in a sheet or blanket.

This happened twice. A few days after the second getaway, we awoke to find Donald missing again. Our father gathered us in the kitchen. Donald was gone, he said, and would not be coming back. We would not see him again. We read the message between the lines, and shed no tears.

OUR FIRST house pet was a cat. I don't remember how it came to join us or what its name or gender was. It was not with us long. It would not stop leaping up on the kitchen counter, where it wandered among our mother's pies and cakes. She loved to bake, and there was always something sweet for desert: angel food cake, graham cracker fluff, brownies. Margaret would not tolerate an animal on her kitchen counter. Very soon, a farmer drove his truck up the driveway and parked it at our side door. My memory diverges here. I believe I was assured that the cat was destined for a more purposeful life hunting mice in the farmer's barn. I also remember, dimly, that the farmer was holding a burlap bag, the symbol of a desperate, watery end for the cat.

Before long, a dog joined us, the result of incessant begging by my brother and me. The dog was acquired from a farmer, and if any money changed hands, it couldn't have been much. Described as a fox terrier, the dog was pure mongrel. He slightly resembled a smooth fox terrier, with short hair and a bulging chest, but his head lacked the shapely elegance of the pure-bred, and this dog was cursed with shorter legs than the best of the breed, hinting at a dachshund in his lineage.

He was brown and white. The top of his brown head bore a white, Y-shaped mark that narrowed as it ran from between his ears down to his nose. We named him Spike.

Spike was neither intelligent nor handsome, and he never went to obedience school; nor would have done so if such academies even existed in those days. He was feisty and nosy. He enjoyed our food and shared our beds. He had an insatiable appetite for mischief and considered himself one of the boys.

These traits are commonplace among dogs, of course, but this one had a characteristic that set him apart from every other dog we knew. Spike smiled. When he came to greet one of us, he wagged his tail, lowered his head, pulled back his lips, and smiled. He did not *seem* to smile, he actually smiled. He showed us his spikey little teeth set in pink gums, wagged his tail, and assumed a posture that clearly communicated his joy at seeing us again.

When he was chastised for a breach of etiquette, he put his head down in a slightly different way and grinned in apology. He never smiled to say thank you when he was fed, nor did he smile at other dogs.

Dogs don't smile, our friends scoffed. But on meeting Spike they had to admit they were wrong.

Spike's other talent was the pants-leg grab. When we ran by him, our jeans flapping around our ankles, he darted in and grabbed the edge of cloth in his mouth. Some children were frightened to be attacked this way, but Spike never missed the pants and nipped our legs. He always got the bottom of the pants, where a cuff would be if we had cuffs, which we didn't. Then Spike held on and pulled.

This dog, which weighed less than twenty-five pounds, had latched onto a running boy who weighed two or three times as much. We could have pulled Spike until his teeth came out, but we didn't. Instead, we hopped a few times on our free leg and then fell down, as if Spike himself had slammed us to the ground. He tugged a few more times at our pants, then released his grip and ran to lick our faces and share a good laugh.

Spike's fierce terrier instincts manifested themselves in another way. He chased cars, horrifying us by dashing into the street after a passing car, running within inches of the front wheel, snarling and barking at the spinning tire. When we could, we grabbed Spike by the collar and held on as he trembled and whined until the car passed. A neighbor said he had a foolproof way to cure Spike of his car-chasing habit. He would drive by in his car and when Spike gave chase, he would open his car door and dump a bucket of water on Spike. We tried it, but the coordination was impossible and Spike hardly got wet. He went on chasing cars.

When we brought Spike home from the farm as a puppy, he sat in the back seat with Pete and me, already happy and looking forward to whatever came next. With this breed of dog, it was customary to cut the tail off, leaving only a stub. The subject came up during the drive. The idea of Spike losing his tail made me uneasy. I didn't want him mutilated.

Do I have to watch? I asked.

Of course you do, said my father, who misunderstood the question. He thought I was asking about my responsibilities in caring for the dog.

I don't want to watch them cut off his tail, I said.

Well, I guess you don't have to, my father said.

Apparently no one wanted to watch, for the amputation never took place. I was often grateful for that when I saw Spike run to greet me, smiling and waving his tail.

In fact, Spike underwent no surgery at all. He was not neutered. This resulted in some potentially embarrassing moments when he mounted our legs, but we were taught that dogs weren't supposed to do this and that the remedy was to push him off with a sharp no. For a time I was only vaguely aware of what Spike had in mind.

In those days dogs were permitted to roam free. Just as we boys were turned outside whenever the weather permitted, so was Spike. He had the run of the town and occasionally disappeared for most of the day. It was a time when a dog could go where he wanted, do what he liked, and then come home with a grin on his face, no questions asked.

## *Learning to Ride*

FOR THE longest time, I did not ride a bicycle. I was still on foot years after my friends were on wheels. My little brother, two and a half years younger, could ride a bike before I did.

I cannot explain the reason for this. Was I afraid of change, afraid of failing, wary of machinery? Did I, like Peter Pan, not want to grow up? There were other signs of this tendency to reject progress. I continued to play with toy guns well into the time my friends were acquiring real shotguns and rifles around the age of ten.

As a toddler, I sucked my thumb, and kept at it long after I was expected to quit. My parents tried such remedies as painting the thumb with an evil-tasting liquid, but I licked it off to restore the comfort of that familiar pressure against the roof of my mouth. On the advice of a doctor, my parents fastened a metal cage to my thumb, a device made especially for chronic thumb suckers that I could not remove. I tried my left thumb; not really satisfying, but better than no thumb at all. Then one day I stopped.

I was unable to cut meat for quite a long time. For some reason I could not handle a fork and knife at the same time. If we were having roast beef or pork chops, my parents had to cut it up for me. Any other boy my age could cut his own meat; awkwardly, perhaps, but effectively. I refused to believe I was able to do it. The prescribed method was to switch the fork to the left hand, hold down the slab of meat with it, and saw off a chunk with the knife in the right hand. Then it was necessary to put the knife down at the top of the plate and switch the fork back to the right hand before lifting it to my mouth. I tried to follow these directions but somehow lost control of the utensils. If we had liver or meat loaf, I cut it with a fork. Hot dogs and hamburgers required no cutting. Fried chicken could be eaten by hand. My mother made a lot of liver and meat loaf.

Curiously, my parents did not press me on this issue. I do not sense, across the ages, the least frustration on their part. From time to time they showed me how to do it, then let the matter ride when I demonstrated incompetence. Neither my parents nor my brother complained about the preponderance of meat loaf and liver in their diets.

At some point my ineptitude bothered me. I took the time to watch how others used their utensils. Then one day I picked up my knife and cut the meat. I was capable, if not skillful, at the very first slice. I just hadn't been paying enough attention.

I find myself wondering, at this great remove, whether my father was worried about me during those last of my single-digit years. Was he concerned about my reluctance to take on the next boyhood challenge? Did he fret because his son was still wearing a toy six-shooter, because he didn't want to ride a bicycle, because he cried so easily?

My mother probably was less concerned. For one thing, I was doing well enough in school. Perhaps her years as a teacher had shown her that some kids are just slower than others.

There is strong evidence my crying bothered my father, at least some forms of it. Sometimes my tears were misinterpreted. Once in a fourth-grade basketball scrimmage I lost the ball out of bounds. I took this as a normal occurrence, but when some fellow players began to console me for losing the ball, I cried in embarrassment. The other players thought I was despondent over the error, but in fact there was something in their concern for my feelings that caused the tears.

At church when I was very young, the preacher made me cry. He was a white-haired old man who shouted at us about damnation and sin. It was not what he said, which I did not understand, but the way he said it—vehemently, angrily, at the top of his voice—that frightened me.

When I got a bad case of poison ivy at Camp Wapsie Y, so bad that I had to go to a doctor and get a shot, it was not Dr. Keith's needle that made me weep. I withstood that, but then cried as we got into the car to leave. I may have been worried that if I cried it would embarrass my father, and this made me so nervous I cried.

Nightmares made me wake up crying. My father came to my bedside and asked me to describe what I saw in my sleep. There were two versions with a similar outcome. One involved a train engine; the other consisted simply of forms. At first the train's wheels, or the forms, moved very slowly. As I saw them moving in my dream I became frightened because I knew what would happen next. Suddenly the wheels or forms speeded up, going so fast that they became an incoherent frenzied scramble. I woke up whimpering. When I told my father what I dreamed, he tried to calm me. It isn't real, he said. It's only a dream. Don't be afraid. I nodded, tears in my eyes.

Then there was what I would call exploratory crying. Just as kids sometimes laugh for no reason, or keep laughing a phony laugh long after the real laughter stops, testing the experience of laughter itself, so I sometimes did with crying.

Once, trying some acrobatics on my bed, I fell backwards, banging the back of my head on the footboard. I was five or six years old. The bump hurt a bit and I cried, and my father came in and saw that I was fine. After he left, I kept crying, not really crying, but emitting a fake cry, just lying there and listening to myself whimper, testing the feel of it. This went on for quite some time. My father came into the room, stood me up, told me to stop that crying, and spanked me with his hand a few times. Now I cried again for real.

Why does he spank me for crying, I wondered, because it only makes me cry all the more? The answer, I tell myself today, is that nobody likes a crybaby. Crying is for sissies.

It was probably my brother's accomplishment in riding a bike that forced my hand. He was two and a half years younger than I, and he could do it and I couldn't. This situation could not stand. My father got me a bike. It was a red Schwinn, secondhand of course, but it was a beauty. Red was my favorite color and Schwinns were the best bikes, everybody knew that, much better than Raleighs.

I learned quickly, my father running alongside to help me find the balance. Soon I could walk the bike up the hill outside our house, get on it, and coast down the street to my father. But I didn't understand how the brakes functioned. I knew that pressing on one pedal or the other would stop the bike, but I didn't know which one to press. As I coasted toward my father, I shouted, Which pedal to stop? and he would call out right or left.

After several runs, my father figured out what the problem was. The brake is always the back pedal, he explained. After I had tested that advice and found it sound, I could ride a bike.

That night at supper, my father asked me what I was going to do the next day.

Ride my bike! I almost shouted.

Stanley grinned and then put his head back and laughed.

## A Father and Son Talk

WHEN I was ten or eleven, the Marion High School basketball team began to win games and attract attention under its new coach, Les Hipple. In an early game in the state tournament, Marion defeated a fierce opponent from Cedar Rapids, a Catholic high school called Immaculate Conception—I.C. for short.

I puzzled over these words, immaculate and conception, neither of which I could define. One day as we were about to leave the house on an errand, I casually asked my father, What does immaculate conception mean?

The question startled him, and I saw immediately that I had made a misstep. Normally, he would simply explain a word's meaning and that would be that. But now he was fumbling for an answer.

I had no idea that my question had thrust upon him the duty of explaining not only a Christian miracle but also the messy details of procreation for everyone but Mary and Joseph. Had I known what I was getting into I never would have asked.

The perfect answer, one that certainly would have satisfied me, would have been for my father to say that it's a way to describe the purity of Jesus's birth. Immaculate conception means clean beginning. Hearing that, I would have dropped the subject gladly.

That response did not come to my father. Instead, he began by trying to discover how much I already knew. Rather than launching into a lengthy discussion of religion and biology, his idea, I think, was to skirt the borders of the issue, avoiding the nitty-gritty as much as possible to reach the answer in terms of my existing knowledge.

He began by asking me questions. Now we were both nervous.

I don't remember his actual questions, but they must have been general. Well, you understand how babies are born, don't you? he might have asked. The accurate answer would have been, no, not really. I hadn't given this subject much thought; it really had nothing to do with me. But I wanted to drive the conversation to a quick conclusion, so I said yes.

This pattern continued. My father asked a question and I responded with half lies, claiming knowledge I did not have. In this stumbling fashion, the matter was resolved, leaving me with only a guilty inkling of what immaculate conception meant.

The ordeal over, we left the house in mutual relief to carry out our errand.

As best I remember, this was the only conversation about sex I ever had with either of my parents.

# III.

# AROUND THE NEIGHBORHOOD

## *Surviving Grade School*

THE BUILDING seemed old even then. Built of red brick, it stretched for nearly a block on one level, long and narrow. Inside, a single corridor led from the front door to the back with classrooms and offices on either side. The toilets were near the back door, boys on the left, girls on the right. The floor of the corridor was concrete, painted I think, and scuffed by hundreds of little shoes. Dust motes floated in the air.

Emerson School served six grades, kindergarten through fifth, with one room for each class. Most classrooms had blackboards across the front wall and one side wall. At the rear was a cloakroom, a sort of open closet with pegs or hooks for our coats and a bench we could sit on to remove our galoshes. Windows lined the other wall, looking out at a playground. On warm days, or even in winter when the room became too warm, teachers opened the windows using a long pole with a metal hook on the end. The sharp sting of cold air revived us in the winter, but in fall and spring the aromas of nature pulled our minds from our lessons and sent us dreaming of escape.

About one hundred fifty students, mostly from the north side of town, attended Emerson. Every student walked to school, even kindergartners. For me, the distance was about two blocks; others had to walk as far as half a mile. Some of these students walked to school, returned home for lunch, walked back to school for the afternoon session, and then walked home again, logging two miles a day in this activity alone.

Kindergarten lasted half a day. The kindergarten classroom was the largest because it held a small stage and thus also served as an auditorium for school plays and assemblies. I remember us as five-year-olds, clustered in one corner of the room, near a sandbox filled with toys. We sat or napped on mats of woven fiber, played games, sang songs, drew pictures, piled up wooden blocks, learned to share toys, and had accidents in our pants. We drank milk from straws poked through the cardboard lids of small bottles.

Kindergarten training emphasized life skills and socialization. We were taught how to properly brush our teeth, wash our hands and faces, and other elements of hygiene. There were charts in the room showing how these tasks were to be done, and upon arrival at school we were required to report on our accomplishments in these matters. Those who couldn't tie their shoes learned how by using laces attached to a block of wood. Numbers and letters were not studied. Some of us could not tell time. One girl had no need for a clock; connected to the deeper rhythms of the universe, she could tell the hour and minute, she said, by watching the falling leaves.

For some reason, a blurred photograph of a few members of our kindergarten class appeared in the town's weekly newspaper, the *Marion Sentinel.* We stood outside the building, against a brick wall, the girls in cotton dresses that barely reached their knees, the boys in jeans or overalls. I stand in the background, a middle-sized boy with a large head cocked to one side as if it were too heavy to hold upright. That head, listing to the left, suggests a wary attitude toward the world, an inhibited questioning. That uneasy posture would show up in many photographs over the next decade, not disappearing until the final years of high school.

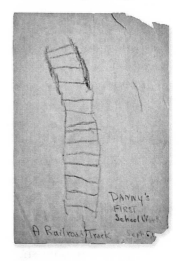

DANNY's FIRST School Work

A Railroad Track

I brought home from kindergarten my first work of art. My creation was simple. Two somewhat parallel dark lines ran more or less vertically on the page. Between these two lines were a series of horizontal lines spaced roughly equally apart.

I showed the drawing to my mother. Oh, how nice, she lied. Is it a ladder?

No, I said, railroad tracks.

Other children drew houses. Did my drawing foreshadow a much later yearning to leave Iowa, or did it simply demonstrate my limitations as an artist? The latter surely.

As we progressed through the grades, teachers emphasized learning by memory and repetition, often accompanied by recitation. Spelling bees were frequent. In fifth grade, Mrs. Snell required students to identify the capitals of each of the forty-eight states. She would not let them leave school until they did it. They exited one by one, triumphant.

We often failed publicly. In one class, we were set the challenge of declaiming the multiplication tables. In turn, students stood at their desks and began, One times one is one; one times two is two. They were to continue until they reached ten times ten—or until they made a mistake, at which point they were disqualified and had to sit down and listen as the next student tried, starting from the beginning.

When my time came, all those before me had faltered by the mid-point, and I knew I could go all the way. The answers flowed out of me in a steady rhythm. As I reached the sevens my mind raced ahead to the glory of running the table—and there I stumbled. Seven times seven is fifty-six, I said, or something like that. I was shocked by my mistake, a momentary failure of concentration, not of knowledge. I looked at the teacher, hoping she would give me a second chance. Sit down, Danny, she said.

We learned to read by sounding out vowels and consonants, becoming familiar with the music of language even as we memorized the many exceptions to the rules of phonics. We learned penmanship according to the Palmer Method. We used a real pen. It had a wooden shaft and a metal nib, which we dipped into a well of blue-black ink set into our desks. Some kids had fountain pens. We tried to emulate the graceful loops and curves illustrated by posters above the blackboard at the front of the room. Following prescribed exercises, we all learned to write legibly. The goals were clarity, precision, and uniformity. We went home with ink-stained hands but we could sign our names so they could be read by strangers.

On appointed days, Miss Wilcox visited our classroom to teach music. She was a small woman wearing a black dress, black lace-up shoes with two-inch heels, a severe expression, and a cloud of white hair. Her tools were a pitch pipe and a device with a wooden handle from which protruded five heavy wires. A loop at the end of each wire held a piece of chalk. Imagine a hand with five fingers of equal length and fingernails of chalk. By backhanding the device across the blackboard, Miss Wilcox was able to draw the five lines of a musical staff with one swipe.

Having made her staff, Miss Wilcox drew dots and circles on the lines and between them. These were musical notes, she explained. She sounded them out on her pitch pipe. She named them, I think, and piped them, and told us to sing the notes. Others in class picked it up immediately, but I could not understand it at all. I could hear that the notes sounded differently when she played them, but I couldn't replicate the sound nor could I remember which note stood for which sound. I'm sure Miss Wilcox then led us in song. I imagine her moving from student to student, placing her ear next to each little singing mouth to assess its talent. I could only drone, hopelessly out of tune, and I see Miss Wilcox's white head shaking in dismay as she moved off to appraise another singer.

In fifth grade I was in a play we performed on the stage in the kindergarten room. It was thrilling to be backstage, where mysteries took shape. I had a good role. I played the father, and to give the character dignity I wore a leather jacket. It was not my leather jacket, but a borrowed one. Although I dearly wanted a leather jacket of my own, my mother considered it a frivolous purchase for a growing boy. The jacket gave me confidence; it lent an aura of maturity and suavity to my performance.

At about the same time, I had a small role in another play. It was conducted by our Cub Scout den in a meeting room of some sort. There was no stage, but we acted on a raised speaker's platform about a foot high across one end of the room. The play was about King Arthur and his acquisition of his great sword, Excalibur. In this telling, Arthur receives the sword from the Lady of the Lake, a mystical figure who reaches up from under the water and hands it to him. I played the Lady of the Lake, or, to be more accurate, my arm did. My role was to hide behind an upright piano and, at just the right moment, reach out with my left hand holding the wooden sword for Arthur to grasp. I believe there was a special sleeve for my left arm to wear. The show had one performance only, my interpretation was faultless, and my parents smiled at me when it was over.

RECESS WAS the best part of grade school. We had two fifteen-minute breaks during the day, and the lunch hour, for those who lived nearby, provided another opportunity for outside play. The town fathers had sited the school well. There was ample room for our activities. A full square block of empty land lay to the west of the school. A sprinkling of small crushed stones covered the ground, where bare spots alternated with patches of tough grass. A crude softball diamond had been carved into one corner of the playground by generations of boys. Older boys quickly formed teams to play there during recess. A much smaller diamond lay to the north, in the remote center field of the larger diamond. This one was used by younger boys or by girls. Children at bat had to be careful: A gnarled tree root jutted out of the ground near the batter's box. Kids running to first base had to hop over it.

Some girls played workup on the small diamond while others organized themselves into cooperative games on the sidewalk and steps in front of the school. They jumped ropes and played hopscotch and jacks. A few boys lingered there, cultivating relationships with the girls.

Other boys gathered in a corner of the playground, unhooked their jack knives from their belts and played mumblety-peg. Sometimes they practiced knife throwing, aiming at trees that lined the curbing.

As for me, I ran with the wild bunch along a small hillside on the west side of the building, a swarming flock of boys caught up in the berserk energy of the crowd. We ran, screaming and taunting one another. Fights broke out for no reason. We seldom used our fists, and never to the face. A fist to the shoulder was often the prelude to a wrestling match that found us grappling in the dirt.

We often came in from recess covered in dust, leaves, and twigs. After what must have been a glorious recess in second or third grade I was so filthy that the teacher, a thin woman in a black dress, was shocked.

Look at yourself, she scolded as I sat at my desk. She was so angry she trembled and seemed about to cry. What have you been doing?

I had no answer for this. Everyone in class stared at me. I was embarrassed, under attack. I put my head down and squirmed in my seat. I did not feel as dirty as she was making out. I had no idea, in fact, that I was dirty at all.

Just look at yourself, she repeated, Just look at yourself.

I saw an opening for a wisecrack. I can't look at myself, I muttered. Some classmates tittered.

The teacher ordered me immediately to the boys' restroom to clean up. My impudent response may well have been the first time I talked back to authority outside my home. It would not happen often, at Emerson School or anywhere else.

Running with the wild bunch on the hillside often included teasing and bullying, and I was surely as guilty of it as others. But in the only incident I can remember, I was the victim. Before school opened one fall, my mother took me to buy new shoes. The pair I fancied had blunt, squared-off toes. They made me think of boots and I admired what I considered their masculine profile. My mother was uncertain; these shoes were not like any worn by other boys at the time. But I insisted, and wore them to school proudly.

The gang spotted my snub-nosed shoes immediately. Like blood-seeking sharks, boys circled around me, pointing at my feet and singing "Dad's Old Fashioned Root Beer," over and over. The phrase was part of an advertising jingle, but in this case it was intended to ridicule my sense of style. Making fun of those shoes became the main objective of recess. I endured the taunts for several days, grappling with my tormentors as they swarmed around me, hoping to intimidate them by throwing them down. But there were too many of them and they were hard to catch as they danced away from me while others closed in. As my frustration and anger grew, so did their teasing. Then I stopped wearing the shoes. My mother understood. The mob had triumphed. I rejoined it.

The childish instinct to attack the weak and different resulted in lifelong pain for one of my classmates—and he was among the bullies. The victim was a girl, obviously from a poor family, dressed in worn and perhaps dirty clothes, struggling with her studies, nervously and repeatedly brushing her hair in class, a fourth-grade outcast. Three boys began following her after school, taunting and chanting at her. They did not hurt her, but were relentless in their mockery. As she walked on one side of the street, they tracked her from the other side.

Take a bath, they yelled at her across the street. Wash your hair. Change your clothes. You're dirty.

Sometimes other boys joined this cruel ritual. The girl said nothing. Looking straight ahead, she endured the insults for two blocks or so until the boys peeled away toward their homes. She never cried or shouted at them, but walked resolutely ahead. This went on for weeks, ending only when the girl's father began picking her up after school. He came for her in a horse-drawn wagon. He said nothing to the boys. Teachers reprimanded them, but they were not punished.

As the boys grew older they remembered what they had done and came to regret it. One of them was haunted by it. "Kids can be horribly cruel," he wrote, "and I am ashamed about what I did to that poor girl. I would have loved her had I not been so cruel and self-centered." His regret was so deep that he attempted as an adult to find her to apologize personally. His search failed. "I have gone to the Lord and asked forgiveness, but I have not been able to ask it of the one hurt the most."

The next year, fifth grade, the girl was no longer in school.

THE PLAYGROUND on the east side of Emerson School held seesaws and swings. Boys and girls alike played here. The best trick with a swing was to use our legs to pump the swing as high as it would go, then bail out, remembering to scramble out of the way as the empty seat, gyrating wildly, sailed back toward our heads.

Seesaws lent themselves to a number of tricks. One was to get off when your partner was high in the air, so that he or she banged to the earth while clutching the handles. This could be done at the request of the other kid, who wanted to experience the fall, or it could be an act of rank treachery. In another seesaw trick, a bigger kid straddled the board and shook it violently so that the little kid on the other end bounced up and down, as if on a bucking bronco. It was almost impossible to shake a kid off the board, but it could be done. Sometimes the little kid let go of the handles and pitched off into the dust on purpose, bringing the game to a dramatic climax.

There were other hazards. Girls liked to play jacks on a cement apron that led to steps going down to the school's basement. This was an outdoor entrance to the basement. The stair pit was guarded by a metal railing with horizontal bars. These bars attracted some of the girls, who liked to play on them like a jungle gym. They climbed on them, made acrobatic moves, and hung by their legs, upside down, hair dangling. This was not especially dangerous if the girls hung by their legs on the outside of the railing, because their heads were only inches from the ground. But if their moves took them inside the railing, they hung above a deep stairwell with concrete steps that descended some ten feet to a concrete basement entryway. Once they moved inside the railing, there was nothing to break a fall.

During an afternoon recess in October, one of our classmates, a seven-year-old second-grader named Phyllis, played on the railing. She had done this before; lots of girls had. But this time she tried an unfamiliar move, or was distracted by the bell signaling the end of recess, or simply slipped. She lost her hold and fell. She plunged head first, ten feet or more, crashing to the concrete below. Girls playing nearby rushed to see her lying at the bottom of the stairwell, her face a deathly white. A teacher came and put a coat over her. An ambulance arrived, and she was taken, unconscious, to the hospital.

A story appeared in the newspaper saying Phyllis had fractured her skull. She remained unconscious for a long time. For three days and two nights she received around-the-clock nursing. (Receipts signed by the nurses suggest that they charged six dollars for a twelve-hour shift.)

The town prayed for her life. Phyllis's friends sent her get-well cards. One had a picture of Bambi and Thumper and was signed by the teacher and each of her thirty-one classmates, who printed their names carefully. The mood at school was somber. "We think about you a lot at school and home," Mollie wrote. "We wish you were at school." Joyce Ann reported that "we learned what 6+6 was" and that preparations for Halloween were underway.

After about a week in the hospital, Phyllis had recovered enough to go home, the newspaper reported. Her condition had improved but she was not allowed to have visitors. Eventually she returned to class, learned what 6+6 was and soon caught up on her studies. The stairway to the basement was screened off with a heavy chain-link fence. There could be no access to the basement from those stairs for anyone.

There was no lawsuit, nor, apparently, any discussion of one. It was not common to blame others for one's own misfortune. "I'm sure the teachers told us not to play on that railing," Phyllis wrote many years later, taking full responsibility. She grew up to become a teacher. She still has a scar on the right side of her head.

## Fancy Free

WITH THE first warm day of spring, when we were seven or eight or nine, we minced outdoors bare-foot, and after a week or so our soles were toughened to the point we could run the neighborhood with-out shoes. Later, as we grew older and our range in-creased, we wore shoes most of the time to avoid step-ping on a rusty nail and contracting a disease called lockjaw, which could seal our mouths shut and cause death by starvation.

Our boundaries were set in the earlier days by the distance our father's whistle carried. He could step out our side door, put his forefinger and thumb in his mouth, curl his tongue in just the right way and send out a blast that covered two blocks, all the way down-hill to the Krugers' house, or even the Brewers'. When we heard it, Pete and I dropped what we were doing and headed home. That was the rule and we obeyed it. Dad tried several times to teach us his whistle, but we couldn't do it, couldn't even come close.

There weren't a lot of kids in the neighborhood. There were the Kruger brothers—Jimmy, a year older than I, and Bobby, Pete's age. George Brewer was one year older than Pete and two years younger than I, but nearly as big. Harvey Sollberger, Paul Elias, Ronnie Achey, and Donnie Schuettpeltz, all younger than I, closer to Pete's age, lived a bit farther away. My best friend, Tom Domer, lived about five blocks away, but he was a fixture in our neighborhood.

WE CREATED play where we found it, much of it filled with action. Inspired by the movies, we played War or Cowboys and Indians often, re-enacting the gun battles we had seen on the movie screen. When we played Cowboys and Indians we took sides, stalking and shooting one another. We died dramatically with spectacular staggers and sprawls. No one stayed dead long. If our enemy fired from a distance, insisting he had scored a direct hit, we could shout, You only nicked me, as we dashed for cover. But if the success of an ambush could not reasonably be denied, we invoked a miracle. I'm a new guy, we would say, then rise up and fight on.

World War II was always with us, a backdrop to our lives. When planes flew overhead, we suspended our games to try to identify them. The back pages of comic books published the silhouettes of U.S. and enemy planes, so we studied the skies to see if the airships above us were friend or foe. My favorite was the Grumman F4F Wildcat, a fighter plane chosen as much for its name as its tough, blunt-nosed profile.

At home, we joined the war effort by saving tinfoil in a growing ball we eventually delivered to a repository in the town park. We saved newspapers, too, until the Boy Scouts came around in a truck to collect them in bundles. I marveled at the dexterity of the scouts, who scrambled over the mountain of papers at the top of the truck, piling them even higher. I hoped to be big enough someday to do the same.

Beanies were in fashion for boys. These felt skull caps had brims folded up and cut in a series of spikes. Early in the war I wore a black beanie with stitching that said *Remember Pearl Harbor*. Sometimes people praised me for wearing it, even though I wasn't sure what Pearl Harbor was.

Newspaper delivery boys, when they came on Saturdays to collect payment for the week's papers, also sold U.S. Savings Stamps. They could be purchased for as little as ten cents, and were saved until enough had been accumulated to trade for a Savings Bond.

We received the *Cedar Rapids Gazette* every day, studying its front-page war reports, topped by banner headlines often accompanied by roughly drawn, black-and-white maps. Many families bought maps or globes to help them follow the war's progress and keep track of their sons, who faced danger in lands previously unknown. Every evening, folks gathered around the radio to hear the latest news of the war, hoping it would be over soon. The meaning of the war came to me through the heroic propaganda of the movies. I fully expected to be a soldier someday.

As we roamed the town, we noted banners hung in the windows of a few houses. A blue star on the banner meant that a son or daughter was in the military. A gold star meant that a son or daughter had been lost. We viewed gold star houses with awe, and were quiet as we passed them.

I was one of the ten thousand Linn County citizens who gathered in Marion's town park in September 1942 to honor the town's greatest war hero. His name was Bill Reed, a Marion boy who joined the Flying Tigers, a famous group of volunteer pilots who flew fighter planes out of China against Japan before the U.S. entered the war. Reed was in Marion at the start of a national tour he would make with movie stars to spur the sale of war bonds. Reed and others, including the governor of Iowa, spoke from the bandstand. I stood with my father, some distance away, on the sidewalk at the northeast corner of the park, not far from the statue of the Civil War soldier. I was six years old. I could not understand what was being said. Then, or later, I overheard someone interpret Bill Reed's remarks: He's saying he won't be back. After his tour ended, Reed returned to the Flying Tigers, even though he was not required to. He was killed in 1944 when his plane crashed.

Our father, in his mid-thirties, with a crippled left arm and two children, was ineligible for military service. He served as an air raid warden. At night, occasionally, as Pete and I lay in bed, we heard the distant howl of the town siren. This was my father's signal to put on his helmet and arm badge, pick up his flashlight, and join some other men to walk up and down the block, checking to be certain that the blackout shades had been drawn in all the houses and that no light leaked out to give enemy pilots a hint that a town lay here. Marion was well beyond the range of enemy planes and rockets, but this fact did not always calm the children who heard the siren. For adults, blackouts and air raid tests were another thing they could do for the war effort, part ceremonial patriotic duty and part rehearsal for the unlikely event of an invasion.

Many consumer goods were rationed and in short supply as the nation turned its production of food, clothing, gasoline, and manufactured goods to supply the military. Some businesses stopped functioning. More than once I saw a sign on a storefront that said *Closed for the Duration*. The first time I saw the word *duration*, I asked my parents what it meant. Until the war was over, they explained. Hope was implicit in those signs: The war would end, we would win it, things we wanted to buy would become available, and the store could open again.

While I was aware that ration books limited the supply of many items, the only shortages that seemed significant to me were those of candy and gum. It was not uncommon for stores to completely run out of Fleer's Double Bubble Gum. When word of a new supply swept through the neighborhood, we collected our pennies and made a beeline to Cira's Grocery or the Farmer's Elevator store. We bought what we could of those chunks of pink gum sprinkled with powdered sugar and wrapped in a little comic strip that seemed inane even to us. Double Bubble was a chewy mouthful that played havoc with a kid's braces and did not taste all that great, but it made superb bubbles.

AT LARGE in the neighborhood, we conducted experiments with whatever nature provided: insects, bird's eggs, garter snakes. A particular form of caterpillar was known to carry a deadly poison. But we were never certain which one bore the fatal bristles, so we took the precaution of manipulating these creatures with small sticks. We sliced earthworms in two to test the belief that each half would generate new appendages and then crawl away as twins. We let mosquitoes land on our arms and begin to feed. We watched their abdomens turn pink, then bulge in crimson. The instant before they flew away we crushed them, leaving their broken skeletons in a splotch of blood.

In one memorable experiment out on our driveway on a hot sunny day, we knelt over a magnifying glass to melt down crayons. We theorized that the process would turn them into chewing gum. We were able to reduce the crayons to a gooey blob, which we thrust into our mouths. The color was right, the consistency acceptable, but the flavor was vile. We did not think to add sugar.

Our backyard led away to an unused pasture, a meadow, really, with tall grass. A stream ran through it and a large tree rose nearby. For a boy with a slightly poetical disposition, this would have been an ideal place for meditation. He could sit in the shade of the tree, his back to the trunk, gaze into the skies, breathe in the fragrance of the grasses, and listen to the trickle of the creek, the hum of insects, and the songs of birds. I do not remember doing anything of the sort. I remember hunting frogs, shooting at birds with a BB gun, trying to leap the stream, muddying my sneakers and jeans on its banks, and pursuing imaginary enemies through the grasses with imaginary rifles.

Not far from this site, my brother joined a snake club. The club may have been inspired by Pete's association at Camp Wapsie Y with a great serpent-catcher named Snake Palmer, a cunning boy who made pets of snakes. Pete's club met where the remnants of a shed lay in a field of weeds and briars. A nearby ditch collected water run-off from a farmer's field. My brother and his friends discovered that a surprising number of snakes—mostly but not entirely garter snakes—had flourished among the wreckage of boards and stones from the shed. The boys began to hunt them, taking them home, and, in Pete's case, putting them in a box in the garage. He could not bring them into the house because Stanley hated snakes, even the mention of them. Margaret had no fear of them at all.

Pete's snake site grew in fame among the neighborhood boys and they formed the Snake Club. One of the boys brought his dog, a beagle, who turned out to be an enthusiastic snake hunter, snapping them up in its jaws if the boys didn't get to the snake first. As the club expanded, rituals took shape. New members had to allow a snake to bite them. The trick was to pick a snake so small that its bite could not penetrate the skin. This exercise was so entertaining that members performed it at every gathering. The location of choice for the bite was not a finger, which was apparently disdained as too obvious or cowardly. Instead the boys offered their exposed stomachs to the snake. The baby snakes did what they could, but no bellies were scarred.

After a few weeks, the boys' interests shifted elsewhere, and the club dissolved. But not before Pete slipped a garter snake into his mother's dishwater. Spotting it there among the plates and suds, Margaret neither shrieked in terror nor shouted at Pete. She did not so much as gasp. She grabbed the snake behind its head, carried it to the side door, and threw it out.

Whether it was a genetic characteristic or a tactic she learned as a teacher, Margaret seemed impervious to our pranks. We could not get a rise out of her with our teasing, and as a result we seldom tried. I once playfully tossed a cherry pit into her coffee. She gave me a look of moderate disappointment, spooned out the little stone, and went on sipping, almost as if nothing had happened. No laughs in that. Except, perhaps, an approving little smile from Stanley.

THE BEST marble game in town had been passed down to us by older boys. It was like the arcade game Skee-Ball, but it was free. We tossed marbles underhand into the slots of a metal doormat that lay just before the steps at the entrance to Emerson School. The boy whose marble fell into the farthest row of spaces, that is, the top row closest to the first step, won all the marbles played in that round. Luck was a factor, but so was skill. Do you go for a direct shot, arching the marble toward the back row with the hope that it will drop in and stay, or you do you toss the marble so it makes a series of bounces before hitting the mat? And what about the most daring shot of all, aiming at the step above the mat, hoping the marble will rebound off the step, roll back, and drop into the top row? We played for hours, our chests bare under the summer sun, our T-shirts wadded up and tucked into our shorts, our pockets heavy with marbles.

On hot days we kept a sharp lookout for the ice truck. Many homes still had true ice boxes, not refrigerators, during the war years. Housewives positioned a sign in a window indicating the size of the ice block they wanted—twenty-five pounds, say, or fifty. The iceman, wearing a leather apron despite the pounding heat, grasped the block of ice with huge tongs, hefted it over his shoulder, and carried it into the house. This was our opportunity. As he entered the house, we sneaked into the truck, ducking under its canvas flaps into the sudden cold. We crawled across the damp, splintered wood of the truck floor, grabbed a small sliver of ice and thrust it into our mouths, relishing the daring theft as much as the cold reward. Then we ran around the corner to avoid being caught. Much later, my friend Tom insisted that the iceman was always aware of our presence and had deliberately chipped off hunks of ice for us to steal.

Many boys liked to play with toy cars and trucks, lining their fleets up on the hot concrete and pushing their favorites around while making motor-like sounds in their mouths. I considered this pastime sedentary and boring and took part only reluctantly out of friendship. Some of these boys liked to stand on a corner and identify passing cars. They could discern a Chevy from a Pontiac, Ford, Chrysler, or Nash, and not only that, but shout out the model name, the year it was made, and sometimes even add a fact about its engine power. I was impressed by these feats of memory but had no desire to emulate them. I preferred studying movie stars. I took greater satisfaction in knowing that the man who played the shy Mr. Boynton on the radio show *Our Miss Brooks* was the same guy who played Cochise in the movie *Broken Arrow*. No one shared my enthusiasm for such arcana.

Like naming cars, fishing was low on my agenda. Stanley loved to fish. He hoped to introduce Pete and me to the sport. He acquired a rod and reel for each of us (he must have borrowed them) and took us to a quiet spot he knew, a tree-lined embankment along a very modest river, perhaps a creek. Stanley helped us bait our hooks and showed us the rudiments of casting and reeling. We tossed our lines into the water and hunkered down on the bank to await a bite. Nothing happened, nothing at all. Pete and I reeled in our lines and looked at the bait. It was still there, untouched. We tossed the lines in again and waited. We stared at the water. Stanley sat under a tree, peacefully holding his fishing rod and smoking a Camel. The contemplative nature of fishing held no charm for Pete and me. We soon propped our rods on stones and wandered off to explore the waterside. This led to scrambling, to shouting, to throwing rocks into the creek, to a hubbub that ended all hope for a catch. It was all over. Dad took us home. Whatever fishing we did in the future would have to be our own idea.

After the war ended, homebuilding resumed and excavations for new home sites appeared in our neighborhood. Mountains of dirt were piled on four sides of a deep rectangular hole that would become a basement. This setup proved ideal for clod fights. One gang occupied the dirt mound on one side of the hole while another gang took the opposite mound. Then we began hurling chunks of dirt and clay at each other across the open pit. For the most part, we dodged the incoming missiles, but there was an occasional direct hit. If a kid took one in the face, it could send him home in tears. At that point, the survivors crept away, anticipating recriminations from the wounded boy's parents. But I don't remember there ever being any.

Autumn brought leaves. We helped our dad rake them into great piles that we moved to the dirt gutters along the street. Then we took turns throwing our bodies into the pile, stirring up clouds of dust. When Stanley set the leaves on fire we were ready with sticks and marshmallows.

As the leaves fell, girls played house by gathering them and using them to shape the walls of a miniature home with several rooms. Some boys played along

with them, but I was leery, very shy and uncomfort-
able around girls. One day a neighbor girl invited me
to join her in this game. I was curious enough to say
yes, but remained wary. I stepped over the little wall of
leaves and nervously entered her domain. She began to
explain which room was which—the living room, the
kitchen, the bedroom. I felt the walls enclosing me. I
was seized by panic. *What does this mean? Where is it
leading?* Without saying a word, I leapt out of the leaf
house and ran away as fast as I could.

All summer, and in the spring and fall on weekends
when the weather permitted, we were outside. For
lunch, we foraged at a friend's house or patrolled back
home for a sandwich, only to go back outdoors again
until our father whistled us home for supper. Then we
went back out to play tag or hide-and-seek, a game
made eerie as the shadows of twilight darkened the
shrubbery and left us uncertain who, or what, lurked
there. We caught lightning bugs until darkness drove
us home, sweaty, dirty, bruised, exhausted, fulfilled.

## Old Lady English

OUT ON our summer rambles, we regularly crossed neighbors' yards if they presented decent shortcuts. We took it as a right.

We seldom lingered on property owned by people we didn't know, but a homemaker in the neighborhood would not be surprised to glance out the window and see a boy ambling past her peonies with a bat over his shoulder as he headed for the Emerson School playground. The backyards of others were our freeways, and we went so far as to walk through their vegetable gardens, going on tiptoe to stay in the furrows between plantings.

Some of the kids in the neighborhood often played touch football on a vacant lot next to George Brewer's house. I always thought the Brewers owned the land and for that reason we were entitled to use it at will. I did not learn until decades later that the land was owned by the neighbor on the other side of the vacant lot, the Baileys. Only once were we asked to leave the property; someone in the Bailey family was ill.

No such tolerance was shown by Old Lady English. Slight and white-haired, she lived in a large house on an oversized corner lot at Tenth Avenue and Eighteenth Street. For us, it was the height of good sense to angle across her front yard on our way home rather than walk straight to the corner, cross the street, turn left, and then traverse the remaining one hundred feet or so to our front door.

Why would we want to do that, when we could cut left, sprint across her yard, leap from an embankment, soar over the roadside ditch, land in the street, cross it at full speed, and be home in seconds?

We did not cross her lawn so often as to wear out the grass, but Old Lady English was upset by our incursions. Perhaps we startled her as she sat in her parlor reading the *Saturday Evening Post*. Maybe she caught a glimpse of our darting forms out of the corner of her eye, then, looking up, saw nothing. *What was that?* she may have wondered, her heart jumping. *Oh, those boys.*

Instead of complaining to my father, an act that would have stopped our incursions, Old Lady English strung a metal wire about three feet high from her front porch to a tree at the edge of her yard, cutting off the passageway. She hung some white rags on the wire to warn us of its existence, but we saw the setup as an attempt to decapitate us.

In our bravest moments, we raced across the yard anyway, ducking under the wire, hoping she wouldn't spot us. We would not do this, of course, if we saw her taking the evening air on her front porch, or walking her Boston terrier named Bean. When that happened, we looked the other way, as if she weren't there at all and she had no beef with us.

There were a few apple trees at the edge of her property, roughly across the street from our house. We passed them often, cutting through a neighbor's side yard on our way to the school yard. We knew full well we were to stay out of those trees, but one day, in the grip of a wicked spell that held us powerless, we dared to cross the street and climb up one of them.

We weren't up there long before Old Lady English bustled out of her house wearing an apron over her dress and carrying a broom. She said nothing when she reached us, but raised the broom and began swatting at us as if a plague of snakes or raccoons had infested her trees. Ducking her blows, we dropped to the ground, materialized as little boys, and ran to the safety of our own yard.

OLD LADY English, we believed, had no sympathy for kids. Little did we know. In fact she was a great benefactress of youth. In 1921, as president of the Federation of Women's Clubs, Mrs. Mary English headed a committee to raise money to purchase a tract of land west of Marion that bordered the boulevard to Cedar Rapids. The land, through which ran Indian Creek, was to be annexed by the town to become a public park.

As the fund-raising campaign progressed, Mary English was its most visible proponent, according to *The History of Marion, Iowa, 1838–1927*. The history, based on the journals of historian Marvin Oxley, was edited by students at Marion High School.

"When many of our townsmen were raising their automobiles up on 'stilts' for winter storage," the history says, "Mrs. English's car and its energetic driver were 'carrying the message' [about the importance of creating a park]."

There were twenty pledges of $100 (one of which came from Mrs. English) and many more of $50 and $25, enough to purchase thirteen acres for $6,500. In recognition of her "potent efforts," Mary English was asked to name the parcel. She dubbed it Thomas Park in honor of her father, Richard Thomas, an early settler who had once owned the land. The park was dedicated in September 1921.

A few months later, an effort was begun to create an appropriate entranceway to the park. But Mary English said no, that a more immediate need was for playground equipment. She helped raise $750 to provide swings, slides, and whirl-i-gigs for children. (Thus giving them no excuse, a skeptic might say, for climbing in her apple trees.)

Mrs. English had started something really big. Two years later, a baseball field was created just south of the park. In 1930, the park was graced with a magnificent swimming pool. In 1935, just across Indian Creek, Marion High School's football field and track were built. Nearby was the town softball diamond, which in winters became a skating rink.

This was a true year-round sports and recreational complex, enjoyed in all its great variety by thousands of citizens over many years—all started by Old Lady English, who hated to see little boys on her property.

THE STORY might end here, but there is more to be told about Mary Thomas English and her remarkable father, Richard Thomas. Their lives spanned 171 years of American history. According to a report in the *Marion Sentinel*, Richard Thomas was a baby when George

Washington was sworn in as the first president of the U.S. (Marion lore has it that, as a boy, he attended Washington's second inauguration, in 1793).

The *Sentinel* wrote that Richard Thomas came to Marion many years later, a prosperous widower, well advanced in years. In his seventies (some sources say even older), he took a fancy to a much younger woman, Julia Jones. Julia was in love with a young man, but the young couple decided she should marry old Richard for his wealth; when he died they could live together in comfort.

But on July 30, 1861, as the nation edged toward the Civil War, when Richard was seventy-seven years old, Mary was born. And Richard lived on. He and Julia celebrated their silver wedding anniversary and the old man still lived on, finally dying at the age of 112 (110 in other reports).

His daughter, Mary, our Old Lady English, outlived her husband and two sons. She died on Friday, February 13, 1959, at the age of ninety-seven. Which means she was more than eighty years old when she chased us out of her apple tree with a broom.

# IV.

# A YEAR IN COOPER

## *An Accidental King*

THE VILLAGE of Cooper sits in western Iowa like a small island sinking into an ocean of corn. My mother, my little brother, Pete, and I landed there in September 1945, as I was about to enter fourth grade. We were told that our arrival brought the population to an even one hundred, but Cooper seemed smaller than that.

The move came because our mother's younger brother, Francis, had been appointed superintendent of Franklin Township Consolidated School in Cooper, which served the few children in town and the far greater number from farms scattered along miles of Greene County gravel roads.

World War II had just ended. Teachers were in short supply. Francis found himself desperately in need of an English teacher and a principal for the high school, and after exhausting other alternatives, asked my mother to take these roles for one school year, giving him time to conduct a more thorough search.

For my mother, it meant a return to her profession. She had been an English teacher and junior high principal in western Iowa for six years after graduating from college. When she married Stanley in the depths of the Depression she had to give up her career. It had been a decade since she had worked in education, but she was ready to do it despite the upset and hardship. She also wanted the money.

For me, Cooper was the place where my love of sports took root, my shyness began to recede, I experienced my first unrequited crush on a beautiful girl, and I received an undeserved tribute I have always treasured.

When the offer came from Francis, Margaret and Stanley developed a plan: Margaret and the boys would move to Cooper for the school year. Stanley would remain in Marion (he worked in Cedar Rapids), but would move to a rented room in the Methodist minister's house. Then they would find a renter for their house. This would be easy to do because there was a severe housing shortage; homebuilding had all but ceased during the war. Grandma Kellams feared that these unorthodox arrangements were a prelude to divorce. But in fact they were designed to shore up the family's finances.

So, in September, Stanley drove the family to Cooper, about 150 miles from Marion. It was a long trip over rough roads in a well-used car. Few autos had been manufactured for civilians in the preceding four years. Gas was still being rationed.

Cooper lay nearly off the grid. It sat on a tertiary road a mile or so off a secondary highway. A paved road led into town, became Main Street for about three blocks, then turned to gravel as it left town, riding the hills through cornfields until it narrowed out of sight. The nearest town was Jefferson, the county seat, a long eight miles away for a family with no car.

We rented an unpainted, two-story house with a sagging porch. The house was on Second Street. There was no Third Street. The view from our front porch was a cornfield. The house had electricity, but no telephone. The only running water came cold from a rusty pump in the kitchen sink. The water's source was an underground cistern that was fed by rain from the eaves. However, our mother suspected the cistern was contaminated by ground water (previous tenants had raised chickens or pigs or both), so Pete and I fetched water from the town pump about a block away. It took two of us to carry the pail back home.

The kitchen held a kerosene cooking stove but no refrigerator or icebox. We kept food cold by storing it in the cellar or on a small side porch in winter. There was no bathroom, only a two-hole outhouse in the backyard. A torn and wilted Montgomery Ward catalog was held by a heavy string nailed to the wall. Mother gave us toilet paper. Many times I looked at the hole next to me and tried to imagine two people using the facility at the same time. For inclement days or emergencies, our mother placed a chemical toilet on a small landing on the stairway leading up to the second story. The smell escaped only when we opened the door to the stairway. We seldom used this toilet and never went upstairs.

Heat came from a kerosene stove in the living room. Pete and I took sponge baths by its warmth during the cold months. A pan of water often sat steaming atop the stove.

Margaret slept in a back bedroom and Pete and I shared what might have been the parlor, directly off the living room. The living room furniture consisted of a few wooden chairs and a bench. Compared to our little house in Marion, this outpost was primitive. No wonder Francis had a hard time attracting teachers. If my mother ever shed a tear over these reduced circumstances, she did so privately.

It did not take long to explore the town. It spanned only two blocks in width and three in depth. The school sat on Main Street, a half block from our house. Immense playing fields lay behind the school. Cooper had one church, small and painted white, on the other side of Main Street from the school.

A clutch of stores, probably three at the most, sat a block off Main Street and a block from our house. A small general store, which also served as the post office, occupied one corner. Across the street was another store, outside of which, in good weather, men in overalls sat on benches, talking. It may have been a feed store, selling farm supplies. My memory calls up another store, but does not provide a description. Was it a small tavern?

Pete and I had the run of the town. We couldn't get lost, and cars posed little danger. People drove cars only to come into town or leave it. Few did either. If a farmer needed something, he might come to Cooper for it, but the town of Jefferson offered far more resources.

Few children lived in town. Our uncle Francis had two, one a baby, the other a girl about Pete's age (he was in first grade). I wasn't interested. The only boy I remember lived in a rundown house bordering a cornfield just up the street. He was a year or two older than I, and a shade or two more soiled. His family kept chickens, and they roamed the front yard, which was peppered with their droppings. I recall an aggressively territorial rooster that frightened me.

And a dog, barking and lunging against its chain. This neighbor boy may not have been a companion my mother would choose for me, but Cooper was a town of limited options.

School was the center of our lives. As a fourth grader, I was in Mrs. Whittlesey's class, which also included third graders, about thirty students in all. Mrs. Whittlesey, who may have been in her forties, commanded us brilliantly, maintaining order at all times as she dealt with the various needs of her students. Third graders sat on one side of the room, fourth graders on the other. I found it easy to ignore the lessons being taught the younger students as I focused on my studies.

We were allowed to work ahead on our assignments, and I took to it eagerly, laboring in pencil at a card table in our bedroom. One day, with a pile of completed homework on the table, tragedy struck. I spilled a bottle of soda pop, soaking pages of arithmetic problems. I howled in terror and watched the pop spread over the papers. My mother rushed in and picked up the bottle to stop the spillage. My distress was so great I had not even thought to do that. We surveyed the damage. Some of the pages could be saved. Others would have to be redone. But the real lesson was this: When you spill something, pick it up right away.

ON SATURDAYS, sometimes, our mother allowed us to go to the general store for a bottle of pop. She gave me a quarter, told me to take Pete, and reminded me that I was to return with fifteen cents in change. We went. I stepped up to the counter, presented my quarter to the woman who ran the store and asked for change, two dimes and one nickel, please. The woman gave them to me. I picked up the coins. After Pete and I conferred, I ordered one root beer and one strawberry pop. I then picked out a dime I had just been given and pushed it across the counter to the woman to pay for our drinks. I did this on several Saturdays—presented a quarter, asked for change, and then placed the order—until the woman lost patience and told me just to order the pop and she would give me the proper change. I may have been a whiz at fourth grade arithmetic, but this shortcut had never occurred to me.

I WAS innocent in the ways of the world, but I was a good student—except in music. I could not read music. I could not make musical sounds. I could hear differences in the notes when music played, but I could not replicate them—or even approximate them.

Early in the school year, the music teacher, a sweet young woman, had each of her students sing "Old Black Joe." The song was chosen because it was very easy to sing. Anyone could do it. I couldn't. The teacher cut me off after a verse or two. She gave me a *U* on my report card—*U* for unsatisfactory.

My mother, the school principal, had a talk with the teacher. The gist of it was this: The boy can't sing. Neither you nor anyone else can do anything about it. He at least tried to sing. Giving him a *U* will only undermine his fragile sense of confidence. Please keep that in mind in the future, my mother advised. (Or so I imagine.) After that, although my singing remained woefully off key, I got an *S* in music at each marking period to go along with an *A* or *B* in academic subjects.

WE MADE occasional shopping trips to Jefferson. I'm not sure how we got there, because we didn't have a car and Margaret did not drive. Perhaps her brother took us. Whatever objectives my mother had in mind have been forgotten, but I'm sure her goals were practical, involving the acquisition of grocery items, clothing, or other necessities. The highlight of the trip, however, was a visit to the soda fountain at Louie's Candy Kitchen. Here, my mother ordered a chocolate malted milk and I discovered what must have been one of Louie's specialties: a cherry ice cream soda. Cherry syrup, tart and sweet, lots of black cherry ice cream, and just the right amount of carbonated water jetted into the mix with such force that it stirred up the syrup and raised a pink foam to the top of the glass. To be enjoyed slowly using a straw and long-handled spoon.

ON ONE of my first days of school, I joined a game of pickup basketball in the school's tiny gym. I had never played on a real basketball court before. Almost immediately I fumbled a pass and it went out of bounds. This disgusted me and I made a face. An older boy was sympathetic. Oh, that's all right, he said. Don't worry about it. You're doing fine. His kindness startled me so much that tears came to my eyes. Now others thought I was crying over the lost ball. It's okay, they said, and patted me on the back. Their concern for my feelings was so embarrassing that I began to truly cry and had no choice but to leave the game.

Early in the high school basketball season I went to a game by myself. I would not get lost. I could see my house from the front of the school. I had never been to a real game before. Mother gave me a dime for admission and maybe a nickel for popcorn. At halftime, most of the spectators got up from their seats and went outside. I joined the exodus, thinking it was some sort of requirement. *Was the game over? Why were we all standing around outdoors?* Some smoked cigarettes, but not everyone. After a while, people started going back into the school building. I froze in confusion. I did not know *how* to go back at halftime. *Did I need another ticket?* I had no money. *What was the requirement for re-entry?* I had no idea. All these people knew, but I didn't. I did not want to get caught doing something wrong. I watched everyone go back inside. I stood alone in the dark for a while, looking at the lights shining from the gym windows, and then I went home. Oh, is the game over already? asked my mother. No, I said, I left.

The playing fields at the school in Cooper were vastly larger than the one at Emerson School in Marion, and we all, girls and boys, played sports and sport-like games. Girls in Marion had tended to play separately from the boys, but here they heartily took part in Red Rover (Come Over) and Fox and Geese. I had never played those games before. In Red Rover, an individual is called to run at a chain of players holding hands, hoping to break through. Fox and Geese is a lively tag-like game played on a large wheel-and-spoke design we stamped in the snow. Here the fox attempts to tag a goose before it can safely reach home in the center of the wheel.

We played baseball—that is, hardball, not softball, the only game permitted at Emerson—on a real diamond behind the school. Although I was unskillful, I began to enjoy sports for the first time.

Our dad came to visit us when his schedule permitted. It was a long drive in an untrustworthy car. He always brought us gifts, usually books, and usually books of an educational nature. When he learned of my interest in baseball, he brought me a glove and a ball.

We went to the backyard to play catch. The small patch of land bore no grass. Chickens and pigs had lived there. The ground was pitted and lumpy, barren except for isolated stands of weeds.

We began throwing the ball back and forth, trying out the new glove. Meanwhile, a man who lived next door began mowing his lawn. It was a rich, well-tended green, the opposite of our rude pigpen. As the neighbor worked in the far corner of his yard, his push mower clicking as the blade cut the grass, my father began tossing the ball to me. His throws were soft and came directly into my body so I could catch the ball by turning the glove up or down. Then he threw one at my right shoulder. Instinctively, I reached across my body with my gloved left hand and caught it—backhand! I had never made a backhand catch before. It was thrilling. My father smiled at my success.

As the game of catch continued, my father alternated throws to my body and then off to my right, and I snagged each one. Then he told me how to move my left foot, how to step across my body with it, giving me even more range for backhand stabs. The man pushing his mower was now about ten feet away, working near the white wire fence that separated our properties. I hoped he would stop his work and praise my new talent. But he ignored us, even as I kept glancing his way.

Well, that's too bad, I thought, but now I know I can play this game.

MIDWAY IN the school year, I acquired an autograph book. I asked my mother to write something on the first page, and it was so tender and loving that tears came to my eyes; she never talked that way. Then I asked my teacher to write in the book. When she returned it, I read: "Smooth seas never made a good mariner. Remember that when life seems rough sometimes. Mrs. Whittlesey."

A girl who sat near me printed in rough pencil strokes: "Best wishes on your girlfriend." The preposition *on* confused me, but so did the sentiment itself. I had no girlfriend and no prospects. I mulled this entry for some time, then decided she meant it as a wish to be activated in the distant future, when, through some process I had yet to discover, I actually did have a girlfriend.

This is not to say that I didn't admire a certain girl. Oh, I did. Her name was Margaret Nipps. She had red hair. She was beautiful, haughty, and cool. She paid no attention to me. I kept my admiration a secret from everyone. It seemed to be the only thing to do.

Margaret Nipps was so glamorous that she even had a fur coat—a fake-fur jacket, actually, white with streaks of gray. This was astonishing apparel in a school where boys wore work shirts, patched jeans or overalls, girls wore cotton dresses (some of them made from flour or seed bags), and everyone but Margaret Nipps wore woolen coats, many of them hand-me-downs. She must have been cold in that fur jacket, which barely came to her waist, but she was stunning, more sophisticated than any girl I had ever seen, and almost unapproachable.

Only once did I hint at my feelings. We were playing a spontaneous game on the steps at the school's side door. The person who was "it" had to stand below the steps, then run up and tag someone who would then become it. Margaret stood on the top step. I raced up and touched her left arm, just above her wrist, feeling for a moment that amazing fur and, inside that, her arm, her very arm.

And that was it.

Then came spring and the last days of school. Mrs. Whittlesey decided the class would have a maypole dance. The school flagpole would be the maypole. Paper streamers of various colors would be hung from the pole. A Queen of May would be chosen. She would stand by the pole while the rest of us, each holding a streamer, marched around the pole, intertwining the streamers as we went.

Margaret Nipps was of course chosen to be queen. On the day of the event, she took her place near the flagpole wearing a paper crown and some sort of cape. As the rest of us began to take streamers I stood at the back of the line. When my turn came, all the streamers had been taken. I was the odd man out.

Mrs. Whittlesey made a battlefield decision. She told me to go stand next to Margaret Nipps. To my astonishment I had become the King of May. I stood beside the queen in my plaid flannel shirt buttoned up to the chin as our classmates circled around us. I did not look at Margaret or speak to her. I sensed her near me, almost shoulder to shoulder. I rejoiced in regal silence. This superb turn of events, completely unexpected, was nevertheless altogether fitting and proper. I was where I longed to be.

When I told my mother that I had been King of May, she corrected me. She had witnessed the ceremony. No, she said, you weren't really the king. There is no King of May, only a queen. You had been placed next to the queen because there weren't enough streamers. My mother did not say this cruelly, only as a matter of fact; probably to quell any embryonic tendency toward conceit and boastfulness I might have been exhibiting.

Even after we left Cooper and returned to Marion she reminded me several times that my moment of glory had come about only by accident and that I should make no assumptions of inherited royalty.

I had to admit she was right. But silently I thought, and still think: Mother, I stood at the maypole, partnered with the queen, the most beautiful girl in the class, as all the others danced around us. I could have been mistaken for a king.

# V.

# A GUN AT MY SIDE

## *Shots in the Dark*

THE IDEA we shared was to sneak our guns into the movie theater and shoot the bad guys.

Several of us did it, more than once, and it was a lot of fun once we got inside, past the ticket seller and the ticket taker. We were about ten years old, or maybe one or two years younger, because at ten some boys started owning real guns. I was always slow to take up new things and had no desire to own a .410 shotgun or .22-caliber rifle. I was into cap pistols, and looked forward to owning a Red Ryder Daisy BB gun.

So on Saturday mornings, before the matinee at the Marion Theatre, I examined my collection of toy pistols. I had two favorites. One was a true six-shooter cap pistol, a rarity, perhaps unique in my circle. Its barrel was engraved silver, the handle made of fake pearl, a beauty I acquired through hard bargaining in the black market of boyhood.

The revolver was too precious to take to the movies. What if it were confiscated? Instead I chose another six-shooter, this one an utter fraud, since it did not shoot caps. It was made of plastic, but had a long, black, mean-looking barrel and a handle the color of rust or dried blood. When I pulled the trigger the hammer snapped, which meant that the gun delivered action with little sound. It was a good choice for the movies.

On the half-mile walk to the theater, I carried my pistol under my shirt, its handle tucked into my left armpit. In cooler weather, when jackets were necessary, it was easier to conceal the weapon. Actually, I did not know whether toy guns were forbidden at the movies, and a good case could be made that they were not, but I wasn't taking any chances.

A dime placed nonchalantly on the counter for the ticket seller in her glass booth. The ticket received, carried a few feet and handed—with no eye contact—to the older boy who manned that station. A few quick strides across the small lobby and then a rush down the darkened aisle. Into a seat, its back a rough, ribbed fabric.

As the lights dim, I take the pistol in my right hand and hold it in my lap.

The double-feature on Saturdays often paired a war movie with a western. Both taught heroism and manliness in the face of deadly force. In war movies, guns were needed to save the world from maniacal enemies bent on our total destruction. These movies also taught us about honor, courage, and sacrifice, the duties men owed each other. World War II was the good war, and we fully expected to become soldiers and fight for our country.

In western movies, guns were needed to deal justice to bad guys, murderers, horse thieves, bullies, and Indians. Sometimes the Indians were the good guys, and even when they attacked a wagon train or a stagecoach, there was something admirable about them.

There was usually a lot of shooting at the Saturday matinees, except in movies starring Gene Autry or Roy Rogers. These singing cowboys taught fair play. Instead of killing bad men, they shot the guns from their hands and subdued them with their fists. By itself, I would have considered this acceptable entertainment, but Gene and Roy insisted on interrupting the action at awkward intervals to burst into song. I vividly remember Gene, perched on his horse, wearing an indecently fancy shirt, strumming his guitar, and warbling piteously. These guys were embarrassing facsimiles of true cowboys. Hopalong Cassidy also taught fair play and drank sarsaparilla (whatever that was), but he wore a black hat and a black glove on his left hand, and he didn't sing.

There were other, tougher cowboys, such as Lash LaRue, the king of the bullwhip, and Randolph Scott, who looked the part but tended to slug bad guys with a sweeping right hand that looked wimpy. There were many cowboy heroes. Towering above them all was John Wayne in his anger, brutality, and lack of introspection.

Before the movies started, there was always a cartoon, and often two, in which Tom and Jerry, or Wile E. Coyote and the Roadrunner, or Elmer Fudd and Bugs Bunny raced through the latest madcap installment in their chaotic lives. We hooted our approval when "the comics" came on. Kids ran up and down the aisles, shouting and spilling popcorn. Management intervened only if a fight broke out.

When the featured movies began, action exploded on the screen, filling the theater with the sounds of gunfire, martial music, and the screams of the audience. I raised my pistol and took aim, clicking away at the enemies of justice, who dodged and fired back. I seldom hit anyone, at least not so they noticed. An exception came when Indians attacked on horseback. Here, a well-timed shot could knock an Apache right off his pinto.

But we had been in the thick of it, and after the movies ended the images danced in our minds. We were transformed. We went home and pretended we were the good guys in a western shootout, uncannily accurate as we plugged desperados hidden on roof tops, behind barrels, or under wagons. Or we were good soldiers, fatally surrounded in the jungle, crouching behind a machine gun, running out of ammunition as we tried to hold off a banzai attack by the Japanese. As the music soars, the smoke from the gun billows up to fill the screen. It envelops the soldiers until they disappear as if behind a cloud, and the words *The End* emerge out of the haze.

## *One Boy's Arsenal*

A BOY'S first gun was often a wooden pistol with no moving parts, its handle splintered, its paint peeling. Metal was needed for World War II. Plastic was all but unheard of.

Later acquisitions were various pistols made of cheap metal, probably tin, secondhand, rusty in places, some with working triggers that made a clicking sound.

As the war ended plastic pistols came on the market. The best I owned, the one I took to the movies, bore a slight resemblance to a Colt .45.

Cap pistols were treasures. They supplied their own little bang and a rewarding puff of smoke. Cap pistols and caps were hard to come by, either because of the war or because caps were illegal, or simply because they were frowned on by store owners. But we got them anyway.

The most common variety of caps came with little spots of explosive powder dotted on a roll of red paper, scores of caps per roll. The pistol had a mechanism that fed the roll from inside the gun up past the hammer as the shooter pulled the trigger. When the system worked, it could be thrilling, producing a string of explosions and a small cloud of metallic haze. But it did not always work as it should. The paper strip often broke or jammed, and the feeder mechanism did not always place a cap properly. The guns often misfired, a frustrating experience in the midst of a shootout.

The best cap gun ever was a true six-shooter. Its caps, hard to find, came not in rolls, but on a disk. Each small red circle contained six caps. The disk fit on the cylinder of the pistol, which rotated authentically after each trigger pull, giving me exactly six shots, and not one more, before I had to reload. It was excellent for realistic play and perfect for Russian roulette. I acquired a fine leather holster with rawhide straps at the bottom to tie around my leg. I became a fast-draw artist and wore the gun everywhere until my friends, who were graduating to shotguns and rifles, began to regard me strangely.

Rubber-band pistols were the first guns we owned that actually shot something. The projectile often was a band of rubber cut from an inner tube. The pistol itself was a hunk of wood in the shape of a long-barreled handgun or a sawed-off shotgun. A wooden clothespin or similar gripping device was the firing mechanism, nailed to the back of the handle. We hooked the shooting band over the barrel of the gun and stretched it back to secure it in the pin. When the pin was pressed open, it released the band, which flung itself off the gun. It was hard to hit anyone or anything with these crude weapons. A reasonably aware intended victim could simply step aside and watch the band lose energy and fall flapping to earth.

Water pistols emitted a puny stream. The powerful soakers that could shoot gouts of water over great

distances would appear in a time beyond our child-
hoods. Our water pistols, which we also called—and
accurately so—squirt guns, sent such little water over
such short distances that we did not hesitate to use
them indoors—until, of course, our father caught
us and sent us outside. He did not like these little
plastic toys, probably because we shot at each other
with them.

Many boys, and even a few girls, owned jack knives,
typically with black handles and at least two blades.
They were tucked into a pocket or hung from a belt
loop. Carrying a knife was practically a fad for a time,
like having a yo-yo, and we took them to school, where
they were tolerated by those in charge. It was incon-
ceivable that they would ever be used in a fight. A few
boys could whittle. We sometimes played mumblety-peg. One version of the game involved throwing the
knife near a competitor's foot. If it stuck in the ground,
he had to move his foot to that spot. The game continued until one player could no longer extend his strad-
dle to reach the knife. I distinctly remember playing
the game on the school grounds, but can't swear that
school was in session at the time.

At some point I also owned a "sheath knife," a
dagger I wore in a brown leather sheath hung from
my belt on my left hip. It was not real, but a plastic
replica. Any moviegoer understands why John Wayne
needed a weapon like this, but for me it was basically
a fashion accessory.

I was once wounded by a knife. David McCalley
thrust his jack knife at me in play. I had been studying
boxing moves, and raised my left arm as if to block a
blow. The blade sliced the side of my wrist. We looked
at the gash and the blood, David and I, and I scooted

through his backyard, descended a neighbor's driveway and crossed the street to my house. There, my mother decided against seeking medical help and bound up the cut. It left a one-inch scar. As punishment, David may have been required to briefly forfeit possession of his knife, although I was as much at fault as he.

## *Rites of Passage*

IN THE beloved movie, *A Christmas Story*, little Ralphie gets his longed-for Daisy Red Ryder BB gun at the age of nine and remembers it as his best present ever.

It was no surprise when I received mine at about the same age. Boys got BB guns; it was part of growing up. The Red Ryder was marketed as something between a toy and a weapon, suitable for children. Carelessly used, it could inflict damage, especially to the eyes, but it wouldn't kill anyone.

I was happy to have the gun, but was distressed at how much effort it took to cock the lever, which set a spring mechanism that compressed the air that sent the BB flying when the trigger was pulled. There was no way to cock the gun with a quick flick of the wrist, keeping the gun in firing position, the way cowboys did it in the movies with their Winchester rifles. Instead, I had to lock my knees together, place the stock of the gun under them, and pull the lever up with both hands. This was an inelegant way to load a rifle.

I wanted a pump-action BB gun, and I wanted it badly enough that my father found one. It was second-hand, but it worked wonderfully and was unique among my friends. It was still difficult to cock, but I could do it by setting the stock against my inner thigh and pulling the pump down with both hands. This was not as simple as working a pump-action shotgun, but it was a definite improvement over the graceless contortion required by the Red Ryder model.

The gun came with the strict and often repeated instructions by my father never to so much as aim it at another person, let alone shoot at one. I disobeyed several times. The first came when Bobby Kruger taunted me. He was sitting in his driveway, about twenty feet from my position on the sidewalk. I decided to fire a warning shot from the hip, planning for the BB to ping off the garage door behind him. Instead, it hit him on the left shoulder. He was not hurt by it, but I was shocked that the pellet came so close to his face. I could have put his eye out. I felt remorse and relief. God had done me a favor, I thought, and I will never shoot at another person again.

Then I heard about the BB gun fights in the bluffs, a wooded hillside south of town. Here teams of boys arranged to meet and prowl through the trees, firing their BB guns at one another under rules of engagement I cannot recall. I remember scrambling in the semi-darkness of deep shade, exchanging shots with my foes—and being afraid I might put a BB in another boy's eye or that he might do the same to me. If this was warfare, I wanted no more of it. I was glad when it ended, and I never went back.

I USED my BB gun mostly for target practice, shooting at tin cans, rotten apples, paper targets tacked to a tree—anything that would give evidence of being hit. I hunted rarely. The rule among our clan forbade the shooting of song birds, but sparrows were considered fair game. I may have shot a few, but the little birds were so fearless that a boy with a gun could walk within ten feet of them. Killing one at that range wasn't hunting, it was murder.

Once I patrolled the meadow behind our house and saw a redwing blackbird perched on some tall grass. It was an impossible shot at that distance. A BB does not fly true and will be diverted by even a breeze. But I took aim and fired anyway. I could see the copper-colored missile curve as it left the barrel, then disappear. Suddenly the bird dropped to earth without a flutter. I hurried ahead and found the bird. It was a corpse, the lovely model of a bird. It had been hit squarely in the head. I did not marvel at my marksmanship. Instead, I pitied the blackbird, killed by accident, and I decided to stop shooting at birds.

I put aside this vow some months later, when a woman who lived down the street asked me to deal with an infestation of starlings in the trees behind her house. She would pay me a dime for each one I killed. I spent hours under that tree, firing at the quarrelsome birds. I hit not one of them. Finally, I had to go to the woman, confess my incompetence, and slink home in disgrace.

It was probably about this time that starlings by the thousands invaded several blocks near Twelfth Street and Eighth Avenue. "Every morning the sidewalks were covered with white and the odor was unbearable," wrote John Vernon, who lived in the neighborhood. One day, Karl Kendall, who owned the hardware store, assembled a collection of shotgun shells and invited every man in Marion who owned a shotgun to gather in the afternoon as the starlings came in to roost and then come back early the next morning before they awoke.

Men lined the streets for three blocks, one in front of each house. At the agreed time, they started blasting. The uproar was enormous. One man pulled both triggers of his double-barreled shotgun simultaneously, bringing down about a dozen birds. When the firing was over, the streets and lawns were littered with small black bodies, branches, and shredded leaves. Neighborhood boys were told to go among the carcasses and wring the necks of the wounded. After a few days of slaughter, the birds went away and did not come back.

MY NEXT gun was a BB pistol. It was black with a long barrel and looked sinister, faintly like a German luger. In fact, it was nearly harmless. It shot a tiny black BB, much smaller than those used in rifles. When fired, the pellet came out at velocity so low that I could shoot it into the palm of my hand and feel only a slight sting. It was good for target practice, nothing more.

One afternoon, my pistol at my side, I was lounging in the town park with a friend when Johnny Marks (not his real name) came by. He was setting off on his newspaper route, his bag stuffed with papers and slung over his shoulder. Marks and I were not friends by any means. He was a little guy, and mouthy to the point of meanness. I remembered him using his small stature to get into the movies at the kids' price, even though he was older than twelve at the time. He crouched down as he approached the ticket-seller, reaching up to push his dime on the counter when the price should have been a quarter. I found this offensive. I don't know what he thought of me, but it wasn't flattering.

As Johnny walked by us in the park that day, headed for his paper route, I asked him if we could see the headline on the newspaper. Johnny said hell no and kept on walking. I shot him with the BB pistol. Just as I intended, the BB hit his canvas paper bag, making only the slightest plop. Marks turned at the small sound and saw me with the pistol. I pinged his bag again. He looked at me briefly and continued on his way.

Marks's route took him past the police station, and soon two cops in plain clothes—that is, work shirts and khaki trousers—came up and took me into custody. They walked me back to the police station. One of them asked me a few questions and offered a lecture on gun safety while the other played with my BB pistol. He was testing its power by shooting it at pages of a *Coronet* magazine. He held the pages up with one hand and tried to shoot a BB through them with the other. The pages and the gun barrel were about ten inches apart. The BB could penetrate two pages, but not four. The officer was having a great time doing this, chuckling and shooting at the pages in his hand. The whole routine humiliated and angered me; it was plain to see the gun was harmless and that Marks was a rat.

The cop said I could go but that the police would keep my pistol for a while. I could come back in two weeks and get it. When I told my parents about it, they said that the punishment was just.

I never went back to the police station. I was too embarrassed. My father asked me about it a couple of times, and I said I didn't want the gun anymore. He seemed to think that was a good idea.

AS I approached the age of twelve, a nervous tension developed between my father and me. He knew, as I did, that owning and using a real gun was part of the passage into adulthood, a time for special bonding between father and son. However, he was not a fan of guns or hunting and may have been reluctant to encourage me in that direction. On the other hand, he may have suspected that I was something of a sissy, because I was very shy, prone to tears at odd moments, and slower than my peers to take up new pursuits, such as riding a bike or holding hands with girls. Perhaps he thought owning a shotgun would make me tougher.

I was not eager to own a real gun. I was more interested in sports and reading. But my friends had guns, so the subject came up, and I asked for one. Sensing ambivalence on my part, my father stalled for a while, and then came home one day with a secondhand sixteen-gauge shotgun. This was more firepower than I had in mind. I thought a .410, the weakest of shotguns, would have been just fine, and a .22-caliber rifle even better.

We took the gun down to the American Legion baseball field for a tryout. The field was within the city limits. It lay between the swimming pool and the bluffs. The high school football field was a few hundred yards away, on the other side of Indian Creek, along with the town softball field. There were no people around, at least none we could see.

We were both nervous. My father said he would fire the gun first, to demonstrate how to hold it. This gun, he warned me, had a kick. It would recoil when fired. Hold it tight against your shoulder, he told me. That way it won't hurt.

He fired a blast into the air in the general direction of the football field. Then he put a new shell in the gun and handed it to me. Hold it tight, he said.

I took the gun gingerly, feeling its cold weight. I jammed the stock against my shoulder, pointed the gun into the air, gritted my teeth, and pulled the trigger. The blast rocked my shoulder back. It didn't hurt, but the jolt was rough, as if a bully had given me a hard push. It was enough, along with the tension I felt, to bring tears to my eyes.

Are you crying? my father asked. Did it hurt that much? He took the gun from my hands.

No, I said, It didn't hurt.

Then why are you crying?

I don't know.

My father looked at me as I stared at the ground.

Maybe you don't want a shotgun. Maybe I should take this back.

I nodded in agreement. I was too embarrassed to say anything. *Why was I crying?*

We went home. He returned the gun to its owner and we never spoke of the subject again.

A FEW years later, after we had moved to a new house that was a little more than a block from the old one, my brother, Pete, became a hunter, and thus the only one in the family who felt comfortable with guns. He was twelve or so at the time. He had learned the rudiments of gun care and hunting from our father, and his skills were sharpened through expeditions with classmates and older boys.

To go hunting, he took his twenty-gauge shotgun out of his bedroom closet, stuck a handful of shells in his jacket pocket and, holding the gun at his side with one hand, left the house and walked through the neighborhood.

Depending on the route he chose, he might take the alley that abutted the playground at Emerson School, where he strode past kids playing on the swings or tee-ter-totters. A boy with a gun in the schoolyard prompt-ed no cries of alarm. Pete went on, passing about a dozen houses until he reached the last street in that part of town. Then he cut through a neighbor's yard, parted some barbed wire in a fence, and ducked into a corn field.

Hunting season was in the fall, so the corn had been harvested and only stubble remained. The air was brisk and the ground was hard and uneven. He worked through several acres of corn and a small for-ested area that bordered Indian Creek.

Pete was after rabbit, quail, or pheasant. When he shot a rabbit, he field dressed it immediately. He took out his knife and made a small cut in the skin of the rabbit's stomach, enough to get a good grasp on it, and then pulled the fur around the rabbit's body and up to its head, which he cut off, getting rid of the head and most of the fur in a single stroke. Then he eased his knife through the stomach lining, allowing the rabbit's guts to drop to the ground. He stuffed the carcass into a plastic bag.

Quail and pheasant were shot on the wing, as they burst whirring out the underbrush. Sometimes he could take two quail with a single shot. Pete could pull off most quail feathers in the field, but getting the meat out of pheasants could be hard, bloody work. This job was typically done by our mother, whose first step involved immersing the bird in boiling water. Margaret did a lot of cooking at home and at work and was not squeamish. She liked cooking and eating game, partly for the taste, but also because it was a low-cost meal.

Several times on his hunting trips, Pete encountered the farmer who owned the corn field. The farmer did not mind him hunting there, but asked one favor in return. If you see any cats, the farmer said, shoot them. If the cats were not going to stay around the barn and catch mice, they were useless. Worse than useless, really, since they preyed on rabbit, quail, and pheasant.

The wild cats were wary of hunters, but Pete saw them occasionally. Most vanished before he could raise his shotgun. But in several years of hunting he killed two or three, perhaps the tamest of the renegades, leaving the bodies where they fell, without remorse.

# VI.

# THE RUN OF THE TOWN

## *Double Feature*

ALLEYS ARE important in a boy's life. They are pathways into the imagination. They invite secret frolic. A boy can run anytime in the back alleys of the business district when he shouldn't run on Main Street. Adults don't patrol the alleys, and few girls skip there. It is always an adventure to travel in alleys.

Tom and I are on our way to the Saturday matinee at the Marion Theatre. After walking about a quarter mile to Fourteenth Street and Eighth Avenue, instead of continuing on to Seventh Avenue, which is Main Street, we cut into the back alley between the two avenues. There are a few houses here with small backyards, but soon we come to the back of a lumber yard. Planks of wood are piled in towering stacks; we hear the buzz of saws, we smell the cut wood. The place feels moderately dangerous. In our imaginations it could be a military outpost or the setting for a gunfight. Weren't we told that a boy was badly injured here, or killed?

We cross the street, sticking to the alley, and pass behind the Carnegie Library, with its small patch of lawn. This little backyard is off limits. We tried to mount a game of touch football here, but got chased off for making noise.

Now we come to the back of the *Marion Sentinel*. The *Sentinel* does a big business in job printing. Here is a large wooden bin where the workers dump excess paper. Always worth a look. I lift the lid. Sometimes there are only scraps, but other times there are rich sheets of fine thick paper just calling out for words and pictures, jarring some creative urge in my throat, or heavy pages of colored cardstock that seem so expensive I want to take them home if only I could figure out what to do with them. I want to keep looking in the bin, but Tom says we'll miss the cartoons.

On the other side of the alley is the southern wall of the Methodist Church, a large red brick building. There is a nook there as the church wall changes shape. It could be a good hiding place, maybe, under the right circumstances, just right for an ambush, depending on which direction our pursuers will be coming from.

We cross another street, Twelfth, and are now in the heart of the uptown business district. (Marion's "uptown" is very small for a town this size. That's because the city of Cedar Rapids is close by, and its "downtown" has many large stores.) On our left is a thirty-foot brick monolith formed by the backs of stores. We can see their old back doors, closed and locked, as if protecting secrets. On the right are smaller buildings and, just ahead, the water tower, the tallest structure in town, with MARION written on it. There may have been, on this day, a crude '47 slathered in red paint on the tower. High school seniors—the crazier ones— try to climb it every year and almost always succeed. The town will send workers up later to paint over the tribute to this year's graduating class, creating a fresh surface for next year's seniors.

These alleys uptown are crossed at mid-block by other alleys, running between Seventh and Eighth Avenues. If we were to take this cross-running alley up to Main Street, we would come out between the Boston Store and Sorg Drugs. Then, looking across the street, we could see an important uptown block: Chesley's Club Royale beer tavern; Storm's Ben Franklin Five and Ten Cents Store; the K-V Café, once owned by my grandfather; the Iowa State Liquor Store; Renfer's Shoe Store; and the Farmers State Bank building, in the basement of which is Harley Breed's barbershop.

This crossroad, these two alleys—the one cutting down from Main Street and the one Tom and I are traversing parallel to Main Street—will appear to me many times over many years as I read stories about small towns. This very alley becomes a setting in Richard Russo's *Empire Falls* about a town in Maine; in that book a church sits about where the water tower is. When a mean drunk staggers down an alley after a bar fight and lights up a cigarette in Kent Haruf's fictional Holt, Colorado, it happens where Tom and I and are standing now.

We jog ahead and cross Eleventh Street. This alley is darker, closed in on both sides for most of its length. The cross alley to Main Street comes out next to Cira's Grocery, a grocery store and soda fountain. Whenever I walk up this alley, passing through the high brick walls on both sides, I feel a sense of anticipation, as if I were about to see a pretty girl I like, or meet some friends who have money for candy.

The town park is just across the street, with its bandstand, its benches scattered about, its spring-fed drinking fountain, the statue of the Civil War soldier, a Civil War cannon pointing toward Cedar Rapids, and the town jewel, Charlie's popcorn stand, pumping out aromatic clouds of hot butter and exploding corn. If there are any other kids I know uptown today, this is where I will run into them. When the disgraced hero of Haruf's novel *Where You Once Belonged* drives back into town, this is where he parks his car, right in front of Cira's Grocery. This is where things start. This is where you hang out until they do.

But today Tom and I do not take the cross alley to Cira's. We go on through the back alley for a half block and come out on Tenth Street, not far from the Marion office of the *Cedar Rapids Gazette* and just above Bailey's Milk Bar. There, across the street, is the Marion Theatre. Tom and I have traversed almost the entire span of uptown Marion without leaving the alleys.

We cross the street and head for the ticket booth, a dime apiece in our hands. The show should be a good one. It's a double feature, *The Show-Off* with Red Skelton, billed as delivering "a laugh a minute," and *Wild Bill Hickok Rides* with Bruce Cabot. It's May 1947, as perfect as a Saturday could be.

AFTER THE movie, Tom and I have options. We can go see my Grandma Kellams, who lives just a few doors down the street from the theater. She will be home. She will be delighted to see us. She will have cookies and probably some candy. She knows I love chocolate-covered cherries. She will make us "cossee," her child's version of coffee: a splash of coffee, a lot of milk, and plenty of sugar. It's a sweet, cool drink. She will find out what we've been up to, laugh about it, and tell us to come again anytime.

We could head uptown and work our way along Main Street. If we had a little money, we could buy popcorn from Charlie and eat it while sitting in the park, watching as farm families do their shopping and teenagers in jalopies cruise Main Street. If we had real money we could get a malted milk. The town is awash in ice cream and milk. All the restaurants offer malts— the K-V Café, Hallwood's, the White Way. We can get malts at the creamery, at Bailey's Milk Bar, at Edison's Drug Store, at Cira's soda fountain.

Cira's is one of the best places for malts. The high school girls working there are pretty to see and they make the malts as thick as lava; the mixture hardly flows through a straw. Cira's also makes an amazing ice cream treat: two scoops of vanilla ice cream held on a pointed stick by a small cardboard circle, then dipped in molten chocolate and frozen hard. You bite through the chocolate to get to the ice cream. The chocolate snaps when your teeth close over it, then the chocolate and ice cream melt together in your mouth. The whole construction holds together, so hard-frozen it is. Even on the hottest day you can eat it all and not make a mess.

But the best place of all for a malt is the soda fountain at the Me Too Supermarket when John Ballard's red-haired aunt is on duty. John is our friend, so his red-haired aunt makes us the thickest, most flavorful malt that can be made and still be called a malt. Her work reaches the threshold between liquid and solid. And sometimes she charges us less.

If we are penniless, Tom and I can go to Sorg's drug store and read comic books. The store managers are tolerant about allowing boys to lounge in the small V-like nook at the front of the store and pretend to be selecting reading material for purchase. We respectfully page through some of the new comics: *Superman*, *Batman*, *Captain Marvel*, *Archie*, even *Classic Comics*, which retell the stories of great literature; usually not starkly enough for us to buy an issue; we are more interested in simple action tales. There are movie magazines, too—*Photoplay* is the best one—that portray the home life of the stars mixed in with a few pictures of starlets in swimming suits and negligees. The higher shelves on the rack hold magazines such as *The Police Gazette* and *True Detective*. These magazines tempt me, but I would not like to be seen reading them. I can get a peek at *The Police Gazette* when I see Harley Breed for a haircut. After about half an hour, we leave. We don't want to overstay our welcome.

Our imaginations aflame after seeing a double feature and reading about super heroes and movie stars, Tom and I go home to play. Tom wants to be Red Skelton. I want to be Bill Hickok. Tom likes the comedy roles, I like action heroes. When we play *The Bowery Boys*, Tom always wants to be the comic lead, Sach (pronounced Satch), played by Huntz Hall. I want to be Slip, played by Leo Gorcey, so I can slug crooks. But on this Saturday, as on all others, there is no clash between Red Skelton and Bill Hickok. Tom and I work it out. We are pals.

## *Haircut*

FOR ALL the time I was in Marion, I went to Harley
Breed for my haircuts. That's where my dad took me
for my first one, when I was about two, and that's
where I went from then on. I have no doubt I cried the
first time, and suspect I did so on repeated trips. I can
see my dad standing nearby, kindly urging me to have
courage, hoping I won't cry this time.

Gradually over repeated trips my howls became
whimpers, my whimpers became cringes, and my
cringes changed to grimaces. I never really stopped
grimacing when Harley Breed cut my hair. Harley
Breed made no attempt to set his little customers at
ease. He handed out no lollipops, engaged in no sooth-
ing assurances. He cut hair. When he wanted my head
at a different angle, he jerked it there. If my eyes wandered and my head followed, he cranked my head back
where it belonged without uttering a word. And thus
our time together passed, Harley cutting and cranking,
and I enduring. It was more a shearing than a trim.

As I grew older I settled on a hair style that reflected my aspiration, which was to become an athlete.
At Marion High School, Coach Les Hipple created

champions and insisted on short hair. Most boys adopted a crew cut, short bristles standing on end. But my hair was curly and wouldn't stand up. So Harley Breed cut it very short on top with a little tuft in front. It was called a "butch," and I wore it for almost as long as I had hair.

Harley Breed's barbershop was in a basement on Main Street under the Farmers State Bank building. The shop was reached by a narrow flight of concrete steps near the south corner of Eleventh Street. The opening was shielded by a cast iron railing. Once, on a snowy winter's day, I came within inches of riding my bike down those steps when it skidded on a patch of ice. Luckily, my bike banged off the edge of the railing and I was able to remain in the saddle and wobble to safety.

The interesting thing about Harley Breed, I noticed over time, was that he had no lips. Well, it could be argued that he had lips, but they were inside his mouth, slanting back towards his teeth, not on the outside like everyone else's lips. So when Harley Breed closed his mouth, I could see only a crooked line in his skin, like a roughly drawn cartoon character. I began to wonder whether Harley Breed, who had no lips, could kiss. Or, if he did kiss, what it would feel like to kiss him. Not that I had the slightest desire to kiss Harley Breed, but it was something to wonder about while getting my head jerked about.

Harley Breed's shop had an interesting feature I have never seen anyplace else. Harley Breed was a cigar smoker. He sometimes had the cigar in his mouth when he cut hair, but more often he placed the wet stub on the counter where he kept his combs and lotions. Thus untended, the cigar often went out. From time to time, Harley Breed, perhaps feeling the stress of cutting a boy's hair, needed a puff from his cigar. Since it was out, he had to light it. He did this in the most amazing way. He put the cigar in his mouth and walked across the room to the wall opposite the barber chairs. There, two pipes stuck out of the wall just above the row of chairs occupied by his waiting customers. The pipes were about five feet above the floor. They were curved and pointed toward the ceiling, like upside down faucets. Harley Breed approached one of these faucet-like pipes and turned a small handle. A three-inch flame came out of the pipe, jetting up. With his cigar stub in his mouth, Harley Breed leaned his head close to the flame and ignited the cigar with a few puffs. He then shut off the flame and returned to his labors. It was enchanting to see fire come out of a wall as if it were water from a faucet. It was by far the best thing about going to Harley Breed's barbershop.

HARLEY BREED'S shop sat on the corner of what was the seediest and most disreputable street in the uptown business district. This is not to say that Eleventh Street was especially seedy or disreputable, because it wasn't. But it had a slightly sordid aura that appealed to some and mildly repelled others. When I was very young, it made me nervous to walk down this short strip of storefronts. Some girls tended to avoid it all together, choosing instead the opposite side of the street, which bordered the town park and was perfectly respectable.

A jumble of painted signs protruded from the storefronts, clashing with one another like too many flags on a windy day. The street ran downhill, from Main Street to the train station, which we called the depot. The store at the top of the street was Kepros's shoe repair, an innocent enough place except that a grinding machine sat in the small front window. In use, the machine howled, the smell of burning leather came out of the shop, and the belts that moved the grindstone gyrated in a way that suggested torture was afoot. The man operating the machine could be seen only in dim outline. Somehow, this was frightening to a kid.

The next three establishments gave the strip its reputation. The first was a narrow beer tavern, so dark inside that nothing could be seen of the interior through the front window. Although its purpose did not change for many years, its name did. I believe it was called Mac's Tap for a while during my childhood. Tap was short for tap room, a somewhat more genteel name than beer tavern. In any case, beer was the only alcoholic beverage legally served in bars. Liquor by the drink was outlawed in Iowa. Whiskey, gin, other hard liquors, and wines for home consumption were available at the state liquor store up on Main Street, across the alley from the K-V Café. Customers were required to present a small blue book that contained a record of their purchases. The purpose of the book was to assure that the customer did not buy more than the monthly gallonage permitted by law.

Next to Mac's Tap sat one of the most popular enterprises in Marion: the town pool hall, a gathering place late and early for good sports, gamblers, and hustlers. The air in this masculine enclave was murky except for the lights hanging over the bright green felt of the tables. Slow-moving fans stirred clouds of tobacco smoke. The official name of the pool hall was

Phillips Cigar Store, but no one called it that. In addition to cigars, the place sold cigarettes, candy, gum, and soda pop. Condoms were available for those who had reasons for not wanting to purchase them from the druggist. The pool hall had a private back room where a man could sometimes get a shot of hard liquor and could often find a card game. Females and little boys did not enter, and many parents cautioned their older sons to stay out. Some boys went so far as to step into the doorway so they could read the scores of Major League Baseball games that came in over the radio and were chalked on a large blackboard.

The next store in the block was another tap room, indistinguishable by me from Mac's two doors away. Many young ladies, and their mothers as well, did not want to be seen passing these storefronts for fear that they might appear to be coming out of them.

Others were not so shy. The father of my best friend, Tom, managed the pool hall for a time. His nickname was "Shine," and he was a fiercely good pool player who enjoyed drinking. Tom remembered sitting in the park on summer evenings with his parents, watching patrons of both sexes go into and come out of the two taverns, the pool hall, and the White Way Café nearby. It was a revolving, free-form party, Tom recalled, and his father told him stories about the celebrants, men and women alike, commenting on their foibles, their problems, and their drinking habits. Margaret and Stanley never gossiped to Pete and me about other adults. Thus Tom acquired a fuller knowledge of the town and its citizens and was wiser than I in the ways of the world.

The Marion depot stood at the end of the block, a symbol of the town's economic stability. Marion was a stop on the Milwaukee Railroad between Chicago and Denver. About one in five Marion residents worked for the railroad. They were engineers, conductors, firemen, mail handlers, office workers, section hands.

Two high-speed passenger trains, the Hiawatha and the Arrow, ran through town twice daily. Their great whistles could be heard for blocks, reminding everyone how big the world was, and how mysterious. It was possible to board a train for Chicago in the morning, go shopping or see a ball game, and return the same evening. Such a journey was unimaginable to me. Chicago, land of the White Sox and the Cubs, was as remote as St. Louis or Brooklyn, accessible only by radio. Even though Marion was a stop on the railroad, it had no hotels. People arriving there usually had business in Cedar Rapids, just a few minutes away, so they hopped into a cab and left Marion in their dust.

JUST AS girls avoided passing by the taverns and pool hall on the strip, some also refused to walk past the iron railing that fronted the steps leading down to Harley Breed's barbershop. They feared that a boy, lurking in the bottom of the stairwell, would be able to look up to street level and peer under their skirts as they walked by. These fears were misplaced. The stairwell was too deep, the angle too narrow, to permit such a view. Take it from one who tried.

## Charlie's Song

POPCORN. THE WONDERFUL smell of corn popping. Charlie's corn, popping.

This was not the stale smell of movie popcorn, large yellow kernels doused in phony butter. It was nothing like popcorn smells we've come to know: the paper and chemical stink of microwave popcorn; the parched and musty smell of corn popped in hot air.

It was a fragrance from another time. Try to remember the aroma of corn popped at home in good oil.

If the smell of that popcorn, that home-popped corn, were music, grant that it might be a flute solo, enticing and evocative as it fills the home.

Then understand that the smell of Charlie's popcorn was a symphony. It blanketed an entire business district. It tantalized generations. It seduced thousands.

Charlie's popcorn was the best in Linn County, probably the best in Iowa, and maybe the best in the world. He used Linn County-raised, Japanese white hull-less corn, crisp and tender, popped not in oil but in butter obtained from the creamery across the street. Milk from Iowa cows, grain from Iowa soil.

People came from all over the county to line up at Charlie's little stand in the northeast corner of Marion's town park. Servicemen, on furlough from active duty, stepped off the train and headed immediately across the park to Charlie's stand, even before going home. The smell of Charlie's popcorn had haunted their memories for months; the first mouthful was a dream come true.

Charlie's stand was a magnet for Marion kids, drawing us uptown to the park where we inhaled the aroma of Charlie's corn and spent what money we had for a taste of it. For a nickel we could have a small white sack of popcorn. Charlie, seated inside his tiny store, filled the sack with fresh-popped corn and drizzled some melted butter over it; we added salt using a tin shaker with a handle that sat on his counter. A larger sack cost a dime. For a nickel more Charlie added a scoop of warm redskin peanuts—a tremendous treat often beyond our means. Charlie roasted the peanuts at his home, giving them a smoky sweetness our mothers could not match when we asked them to pop up the same delicacy. For our beverage, we slurped Marion's spring water from the public fountain a few feet away.

Charlie Carrington wasn't the first popcorn man in Marion's park, nor was he the last. But he was there through the Depression and World War II, so he was our popcorn man, continuing a tradition that began in 1914.

For twenty-two years, every afternoon from April into November, Charlie came to his little white stand, a shed really, about ten or fifteen feet wide, perhaps five feet deep, room enough only for Charlie, a chair, his popper, and his supplies. He put on his green visor and began parceling out yesterday's leftovers, free to greedy kids and squirrels. The squirrels came out of the trees when Charlie tapped on his counter. The kids needed no reminder.

Charlie had a way with squirrels. At home, he had trained one to take a peanut out of his sweater pocket. The squirrel always looked in the same pocket, even when Charlie put the treat in the other one.

After feeding the squirrels and kids, Charlie began popping. His first day on the job was in early May 1931; his last day was in April 1953. In the early years of the Depression, the stand stayed open until 11:00 p.m. The town was somehow busier then. As the years passed, the closing hour came earlier, around 9:00 p.m. On that first day in May, his take was $2.50—the equivalent of fifty nickel bags of corn sold.

Business improved. Popcorn, cheap and plentiful during the Depression, gained popularity as a snack food. When sugar rationing curtailed the production of sweets during World War II, popcorn consumption soared.

Charlie's wife once said that he popped a ton of corn a year. If this was an accurate measure, we are permitted some estimates. Let's say a five-cent bag of popped corn weighs an ounce. With sixteen bags to a pound, a ton of corn yields thirty-two thousand nickel bags, which turns into $1,600 in gross income for Charlie. Even if the bags weighed half an ounce, a ton of popcorn would yield only $3,200 in gross sales. Perhaps there was more profit in the roasted peanuts.

Or perhaps Charlie did it for love. It took a tragedy for him to get into the popcorn business.

Charlie had been a railroad man, working out of Marion on the Milwaukee line, a freight train conductor (or brakeman in other references) and considered "one of the best men on the run," according to the *Marion Sentinel*, whose reports over the years provided many of the facts here about Charlie. (Information is also drawn from the *Cedar Rapids Gazette*.)

On December 6, 1930, Charlie was working with other trainmen to switch cars in the rail yards in Savanna, Illinois. He may have been standing atop a freight car, but in any event he fell across the tracks as the car began to move, and its wheels rolled over his legs, severing one. The other leg was amputated at the hospital. He was forty-two years old.

Depressed, frightened about the future, Charlie looked out his hospital window one day and saw a man walk up the icy sidewalk and enter the building. He was a fellow railroad man, and he had come to show Charlie something: He pulled up his trousers to reveal his wooden legs. The man had lost his own legs, yet here he was, navigating icy walkways. Charlie was immediately heartened. *If he can do it*, he thought, *so can I.*

Charlie went to the Artificial Limb Company in Council Bluffs and got himself fitted with two artificial legs. He spent three months on crutches and three more on a cane until he could walk without assistance on legs and feet of English willow.

By that time he had purchased the popcorn stand from the estate of Pete Kassler and was operating it under a permit from the town. Kassler had been a blacksmith who suffered an injury that paralyzed his legs, and in granting the license to Charlie, Marion's city fathers continued the practice of awarding the permit "to allow a means of a living" to a person with a handicap.

Charlie enjoyed telling reporters about his dealings with the children who frequented the park. Kids used him as a bank, buying some popcorn and leaving their money with him as they played. When they came to get their coins, they sometimes found they did not have enough money to go to the movies, so Charlie made up the difference.

In his role as banker, Charlie once set up a little box for a girl who wanted to save money to buy clothes for school. All summer, she gathered empty pop bottles, redeemed them, and kept her pennies in the box Charlie provided. At the end of summer, he made sure she had enough to buy what she wanted.

Charlie must have been busiest on summer evenings after the war when the high school band played concerts in the park. Folks arrived before twilight. Some sat on the park's green benches; others brought canvas chairs or spread blankets on the grass. They bought popcorn, and the smell of it popping scented the air. A fragrant cloud spread over the park, wafted over the whole business district, enveloped everyone.

The bandstand was on stilts, open on all sides. Little kids loved to romp under the floor of the bandstand, racing back and forth across the dirt, their heads nearly scraping the wood above, delighted to be so small and fast.

Now the high school band took the stage, as many as fifty strong, dressed in white, short-sleeved shirts. As the band tuned up, parents rounded up their children, shooing them from under the bandstand, telling them to sit still now.

Paul Wright, the bandleader, tall and serious, took his place. He studied his musicians for a moment, tapped his baton on his music stand, and raised his arms over his head. The first number would be a Sousa march, a lively opening to the hour-long concert. People stopped talking, hushed their children, and settled back, ready to listen.

In the brief silence before Mr. Wright struck up the band, the concertgoers might hear, off to their left, the soft rattle of Charlie's corn pop-popping like a distant drum, tapping out its own cadence, making its own music, working its own magic.

## *Memories of Water*

I AM lying, face down, stretched out and holding my breath, in water two feet deep. It's the baby pool in Bever Park, Cedar Rapids, and I am teaching myself to swim. I'm six years old. My little brother sits near the pool's rim, splashing. My mother rests on a bench, watching. We have come here by bus from Marion. It's the safest place she knows for kids to play in the water.

I make small, dog-paddling movements with my hands. The water isn't deep enough for a full overhand stroke. My effort takes me a few feet into very shallow water, where my stomach scrapes the brown concrete bottom of the pool. I lift my head out of the water, take a deep breath, turn, bury my face in the water again and start paddling in the other direction.

I do this for an hour, back and forth like a caged dolphin. I'm ready for a bigger pool.

MY FATHER learned to swim in Marion's Indian Creek when he was a boy in the 1910s and 1920s. There was no swimming pool in Marion then. He recalled his experiences in a guest column in the *Marion Sentinel* dated January 17, 1946. He wrote:

"[T]here were always two or three swimming holes [in the creek] and each was always full of naked boys. I learned to swim in Indian Creek when I was six, and I don't believe I owned a bathing suit until I was out of high school and began to patronize modern and antiseptic pools.

"My earliest swimming was done at the 'Long Log.' Each hole had its name and as the creek filled old holes in its bed from year to year, intrepid explorers would always find new ones and appropriate names would be applied.

"'Long Log' was named for a great tree which had fallen and lay lengthwise with the current along one bank of the stream. This hole was about half a mile north of the old fairgrounds, now the golf club. The deep water was at the root end of the log and we used that natural elevation for our diving board.

"However, the water was not quite deep enough for the bigger boys, so with the help of my father and A. A. Hardin, we undertook to build an ambitious dam of sand bags. . . Our dam was a success and probably raised the level of the water two or three feet. In fact it was so successful that it caused considerable consternation and caustic comment at the dam downstream at the mill which was then grinding buckwheat by water power.

"However, this difficulty was overcome, and we enjoyed a long summer of fine swimming. It was at the 'Long Log' that I first achieved swimming success— under water. . .

"My efforts at surface swimming were rewarded the next summer at the 'Willows,' a new hole about 200 yards upstream from the 'Long Log.' It was here that I first conquered the depth and width of Indian Creek, over and back. I thought that all was lost when I made the mistake of 'letting down' in water over my head and hands. However I made crossing safely with my father, my brother, Mr. Hardin, and Harlan Briggs forming an enthusiastic audience if an indifferent lifesaving crew. . .

"After the 'Willows' there was a series of fine holes. 'Grassy Bank' was just below the 'Long Log.' I broke my arm there by diving into shallow water. Ernie and Hooley [Hardin brothers] helped me dress and get home. Hooley went on ahead to carry the message and I was attended by my mother and a group of kind neighbors all the way from the Tenth Street bridge. . .

"The 'Sand Bar' was the favorite hole for several years, and many kids learned to swim there. It had a sloping beach on the east side of the creek, and a high bank over deep water for diving on the west side.

"Phil Crew and I used to swim at the 'Sand Bar,' and I remember how we would come home from a long swim to eat baked bean sandwiches and smoke pieces from an old wicker chair which had been abandoned in our woodshed. Phil and I must have smoked up most of that old chair. Its porous slender segments were much handier than cigarettes made of corn silk or coffee, but the smoke was so bitter and hot that our tongues would almost blister. . .

"Our swimming season was very long. Someone always took a brief and shivering plunge during a soft day in April to find out how the water was. They always returned with goose pimples and running noses to tell us the water was fine.

"However by mid-May the season was in full bloom. Through June and July and the dog days of

August, when we splashed the green scum away from the swimming area, and into the fall, Indian Creek was full of cavorting kids.

"Every day we came home with dirty chins, which is still the badge of creek swimmer, and cannot be won in a pool."

SOME OF my friends swam often in Indian Creek, but I did so only a few times. The hole we swam in couldn't have been far from 'Long Log.' It was a nice deep spot at the northern edge of town, not far from the country club. Someone had strung a rope from a tree, so we could swing out and drop into the muddy pool. We swam naked.

We also visited the YMCA in Cedar Rapids a few times, and swam naked there in its indoor pool. There was a wonderful fresh feeling to it, almost baptismal.

I preferred the American Legion Pool in Marion, a vast playground that attracted kids by the hundreds. As we approached the pool, we heard the shrieks from a block away and could almost smell the chlorine. On foot or bike, we picked up our pace. Not a moment to lose.

The pool, built in 1929, was one of the largest in the county. It had an unusual, amoeba-like shape, with only one ninety degree angle, the result of a decision when it was built to fit it among five large trees.

It was divided into three areas: a baby pool with depths ranging from a few inches to two feet, a large free-swimming area with a depth of four feet, and a ten-feet-deep diving area. Depending on their skill or courage, divers could choose from among four boards:

two about three feet high, one six feet high, and a third ten feet high. (Boards higher than one meter are rarities today in public pools because of liability concerns. Many newer pools have no diving board.)

On hot days in the 1940s and 1950s, before air conditioning, as many as five hundred people lined up before the pool opened at noon for general swimming. Admission prices were a quarter for children and thirty-five cents for adults.

As we approached the entrance, we dumped our bikes on a grassy slope and ran to get in line, edging forward steadily. We passed through a gated area, now inside the fence that surrounded the pool and most of its buildings. At the first outpost we handed our money to a blonde girl a few years older, a high school student, sun-struck and beautiful. All the older boys and girls working at the pool were bare-legged and robust, not deities exactly, but mysteriously blessed to have such extraordinary jobs. The blonde girl gave us a ticket. There was another girl in the ticket office. Perhaps she was wrapping coins. Taking a few more steps, we reached the entrance to the changing room and handed our ticket to another worker, who gave us a basket and a rubber wrist band.

Now truly inside the place, we entered the changing room, dank and smelling of mold, water puddles on its concrete floor. A series of stalls behind canvas curtains lined each side of the room. Inside a stall, we put our baskets on a small bench painted blue and white and stripped off our clothes. Into our swimming trunks, then into an adjoining stall for the quick, mandatory, cold shower.

So eager now, we pulled on our wrist band, grabbed our basket and made for the pool in a shuffling run.

We minced through a small icy footbath containing a chemical to prevent athlete's foot and almost flung our basket at the attendant. We ran into the sunshine, into the baby pool, dived over its rope into the four-foot pool, and came up gasping with joy.

Kids from tots to teens swarmed the place. Young mothers sat on wooden benches just outside the pool, watching their children romp. They pushed coins through the wire fence so their children could visit the snack bar. On cooler days, little boys and girls wrapped towels around themselves and sat shivering and blue-lipped on benches inside the fence. When their goose bumps receded, they plunged back into the water.

A tremendous clamor rolled over the pool, a combination of laughter, splashing water, the bellows of older children, and the squeals of younger ones.

Lifeguards sat on high chairs or patrolled the concrete platform that surrounded the water. They surveyed the multitudes at play, looking not only for anyone in danger, but also for improper behavior, such as fighting or dunking another kid. The threat of expulsion brought a quick end to such conduct. Running children were stopped in their tracks by the blast of a lifeguard's whistle.

There were always a few teenage boys outside the pool, lounging against the fence, resting on their forearms with their hands above their heads, fingers grasping the fence as if about to climb it. They ogled the female lifeguards, tan and remote in their authority, and scanned the crowd for glimpses of swimsuit-clad girls they admired.

Hot weather brought out the girls, who tanned themselves on one of two sunning decks. The preferred spot was near the diving area, allowing the sunbathers to see and be seen by the divers. This was the hottest spot in the pool, but it was small. There was another larger sunning deck all the way across the pool from the roadside spectators.

The boys at the fence could not get a decent look at the girls sunning on the opposite side. There were no benches outside this sunning area; no pathway went by it. It was isolated and that's probably why the girls chose it.

A boy needed a good excuse to go halfway around the pool to be able to stand near the sunning girls, and I could never think of one. One day I spotted a pal standing next to his bicycle and actually talking to some of the girls. Here was my chance. I could approach my friend on the pretext of chatting with him while I feasted my eyes on the bodies splayed out and glistening in the sun. It was a long way around the pool to the sunning spot. I circled around the refreshment stand, quick-stepped past the ticket booth, and made the final right hand turn toward the sunning deck— only to discover that my friend had disappeared. He had pedaled off on some mindless errand of his own, leaving me no choice but to slump back to my bench by the road.

The swimming pool was one of Marion's greatest glories, but it had a dark secret that most kids didn't learn until they reached high school. The pool was restricted; people of color were not admitted. The pool's owner, the American Legion, a private organization, apparently had the law on its side. There were no signs proclaiming the policy, nor was it widely discussed. Many swimmers didn't know it existed; others were dimly aware of it. Many kids in Marion had never met a black person.

## Root Beer: Sweet and Bitter

THERE WAS no taste sweeter than root beer after a long day at the swimming pool, and there was no better place to taste it than the A&W Root Beer stand a few blocks from the pool. It was here that we dipped our eager noses into a foam-topped mug of caramel-colored soda, slaking our mighty thirsts before the long ride home, most of it up hill. It was here that I perpetrated a bitter cruelty on a hot summer afternoon.

The root beer stand was a drive-in, part of an early fast-food chain. Marion's version opened in 1949. It was by no means a restaurant, rather two steps up from a shack. The wooden building was perhaps twenty-five feet long. An awning striped with the A&W colors of brown and orange hung across the face of the structure, partially covering a length of four screened-in service windows. There was no seating, inside or outside.

The stand (we always called it that), sat on a V-shaped peninsula formed by two streets, the largest of which was Marion Boulevard, the main route to Cedar Rapids. Both streets were well traveled, and cars came in from either side to find a place to park. At night, when the Twixt-Town drive-in movie let out, or the stock car races ended at CeMar Acres, cars poured down the boulevard in a line of headlights bound for the A&W drive-in.

Parking spots were not designated by painted lines; drivers simply found an open area. Soon a high school girl in a white blouse and a black, ankle-length skirt approached the car carrying a menu. She was a carhop, a word some people found vaguely offensive.

Each girl had an assigned area, and boyfriends and regulars vied for key locations. After taking the order, the carhop returned shortly with a tray of food and drink. The metal tray had rubber-covered hooks that fit over the car's side window, which had to be rolled not quite all the way down. A brace unfolded under the tray and sat against the outside of the car door to create a wedge that held the tray in place.

When customers finished eating, the driver blinked the car's headlights to signal the carhop to retrieve the tray. If tips were left, they were small, a dime or a quarter. Carhops were paid forty cents an hour.

The Marion root beer stand was a summer place. It was operated by Wally and Dorothy Luedtke, who put in sixteen-hour days, working in close quarters with a revolving staff composed mostly of high school students and a few adults. Temperatures outside soared into the nineties, and inside felt like an oven. Sizzling griddles, deep fat fryers, and a popcorn machine filled the room with an oily mist. Exhaust fans pumped the fumes into the humid Iowa air, where the first whiff intoxicated customers.

Dorothy served as head cook while Wally supervised the entire operation, seeing that orders were properly assembled and quickly delivered, handling the money, correcting missteps, dealing with customer complaints, and urging the laggard to pick up the pace. When boyfriends drove up at closing time to meet a carhop, Wally insisted that the girls call their parents for permission to get into the car.

While carhops sought the shade on the north side of the stand, the south side featured a walk-up counter. It was here that I first tasted A&W Root Beer and at some point shortly afterward committed the cruelest act of the many I inflicted on my little brother.

Because the stand was an essential stop on the way home from the swimming pool, I always tried to limit my expenditures at the pool snack bar to have money left over for root beer.

By the time we reached the stand we were already feeling the heat of the merciless Iowa sun. Our fingertips were still puckered from hours in the water. Our hair, cut short, was dry, but our towels and swimming suits, rolled in a ball under our arms, were damp against our T-shirts. Our throats were parched.

A small frosted mug of root beer cost five cents. A large one cost a dime, which was often more than we had. Only those who had come into wealth could afford a root beer float. A tenderloin sandwich or onion rings were out of the question.

The first sip of root beer was the best. We grasped the frosted handle and lifted the mug to our mouths, stuck our lips into the rich foam, felt the fizz tickle our noses, sipped the sweet brown soda through the foam, and felt its spices run across our tongues. We didn't want to drink it too fast. It was still a long way back home.

On one of those hot days, I approached the stand with three friends and my brother. Although my brother was two and a half years younger and three grades behind me in school, and so far as I knew had his own circle of friends, he insisted on tagging along with me and inserting himself into my relationships. This infuriated me. So I tortured him.

On this day I had fifty cents. As we stood at the counter, the heat radiating around us, I bought a large root beer for each of my friends and myself. Out of some deep, jealous anger, I told my brother he was not getting any root beer from me. He had no money.

The service person brought us our order, and gave my brother a small mug of water. The mug was not even frosted, like ours, an A&W tradition. My brother said nothing and sipped his water as the rest of us slurped root beer, the foam trickling over the sides of our mugs.

I looked down at his sandy head bent over his mug of water. My brother was not crying, just silently and morosely drinking his water. I must have felt a twinge of guilt, for the impulse came to buy him a five-cent mug of root beer. He was my brother, yes, but he was also human. Still, I did nothing. I let him suffer. And I regretted it for the rest of my life.

Many years later, and many years ago, I visited my brother and his family. I brought along a large bottle of A&W Root Beer and asked his forgiveness for what I had done decades earlier. He did not so much accept my apology as dismiss it.

Your being mean to me made me tough, my brother said. He told me to think no more about it.

But I still see that bent head, that water-filled mug in his hand.

# VII.

# SUMMERS ON THE RIVER

## Wapsipinicon Years

*YOU GOTTA get up, you gotta get up, you gotta get up in the morning.*

Did the sounds of "Reveille" awaken us? I seem to remember that they did. Among the counselors there may have been one who could play the bugle or trumpet. So we pulled on our T-shirts, jeans, and canvas sneakers and poured out of our cabins into formation—about seventy-five boys, all present and accounted for, hungry and ready to attack the day. We watched as two older boys unfolded the flag from its triangular shape, clipped it to the ropes, and raised it high on the pole. We placed our hands over our hearts and recited the Pledge of Allegiance. The ceremony complete, we broke for the mess hall as the counselors dragged a few blankets, wet from last night's urine, into the sun to dry.

This is Camp Wapsie Y, a handful of wood-framed buildings strung along a bend in the Wapsipinicon River, not far from Central City. It was only fifteen miles from my home in Marion, but it might as well have been Shangri-La. My brother and I were there because our mother had taken a job as cook. Instead of paying to give us a week at camp, she worked the entire summer—eight to ten weeks, seven days a week, preparing three meals a day for about one hundred people, not counting the work of setting up and then closing down the place. Pete and I reaped the reward of her frugality and hard work: four summers at camp, 1944 through 1947, the summers I turned eight through eleven.

This is not to say that my mother, Margaret, did all the kitchen work herself. She shared cooking duties with Mrs. Hamilton, whose three sons were also at camp, and the two women were assisted by a group of junior counselors—high school or college boys. While Margaret may have been granted time off during the week, she carried great responsibilities and labored long hours. She and Mrs. Hamilton slept in relatively primitive conditions in the cooks' cabin a few steps from the mess hall. They each had a small room, partitioned by walls of raw wood still rough with splinters and threads from the saw. Toilets and showers for the entire camp were located in a latrine on the other side of the mess hall, although of course the cooks had access to running water in the kitchen, so there may have been a bathroom there as well. That the two mothers would tolerate these conditions for four summers was a profound testimony to their devotion to their sons, and we must have appreciated it in the abstract way of boys wrapped in their own existences, for we certainly had a lot of fun at camp, and our mothers knew it.

Wapsie Y had historic credentials as a campsite. A semi-nomadic tribe of Indians, the Mesquakie, had used the area for many years, arriving by canoe and pony to camp there for a few weeks. In our time the land was owned by the Hutchins family and rented out to the YMCA; it was basically part of the family farm.

The camp was set on a ledge about twenty feet above the river. The Wapsipinicon, on its way from southern Minnesota to the Mississippi River in southern Iowa, flowed from the west toward this ledge, then hooked to its right, turning south and running over a length of stones that stretched across the river. This shallow, stone-marked area was called "the rapids." The bend in the river where it turned south created a backwater, a pond-like area with little current. The boat dock was here, with a handful of scarred rowboats and a few canoes. Only campers who had demonstrated superior swimming skills were allowed to use canoes.

We did not have life vests. There may have been a few life preservers—white round buoys—lying on the dock.

About once a summer, some inept campers in a rowboat ventured too far out of the backwater, got caught in the current, and were swept toward the rapids. Other campers shouted about their plight, attracting the attention of the counselors. The rowers, if they panicked, flailed helplessly with their oars, or pulled them out of their locks and couldn't seem to put them back. Their oars waved helplessly as the boat drifted downriver.

But the boat did not reach the rapids. Instead, it came to rest against a cable laid in front of the rapids for just this purpose. The boys in the boat could grab the cable and hold on as some counselors waded into the river along the cable and rescued the boys, who were embarrassed and thrilled by their adventure. The danger was not that the boat would capsize when it hit the rapids; more likely it would be grounded by the stones. The real concern was that the boat might slip over the rapids and continue downstream, creating a frantic chase for counselors in canoes.

There was a small strip of pebbly beach near the rapids, so filled with stones and sandy soil that no tall grasses could grow there. Here we disturbed craw daddies hiding in the rocky shallows and skipped stones across the water, counting their leaps until they sank just short of mid-river. The scramble down to the river and then back up to camp, using exposed tree roots as handholds, was part of the fun.

The buildings and grounds of the camp were rudimentary—no more than they had to be. The mess hall marked the southern boundary of the camp. It was flanked by the latrine to the east and the cooks' cabin to the west. The cooks' cabin overlooked the rapids.

To the north, six campers' cabins in two rows were set well back from the river, fronting a sort of parade ground about the size of a football field, perhaps longer. A flagpole was centered near the river ledge, across the width of the parade ground from the cabins. No parades were held there, but the grass was well worn by our comings and goings, the ground marked by small patches of tough weeds. The cabins were small, jammed with bunk beds. Canvas slings served as mattresses. I have almost no memory of life inside the cabins. I must have entered them exhausted and slept well.

Opposite the mess hall, at the other end of the parade ground, sat the lodge, built around a huge stone fireplace. The lodge was used for activities on rainy days or chilly evenings. It also had a small store where campers could buy a candy bar or package of gum—rare treats in wartime, when sugar was rationed.

A Ping Pong table stood outdoors on the east side of the lodge. I had never played the game and one summer spent hours watching older players compete. Most kids new to the game would just pick up a paddle and learn by trial and error. But I was wary. By watching, I learned how to keep score, noted the different ways to grip paddles, learned the basic forehand and backhand strokes, and developed insights into the strategy of the game. After several weeks of research I picked up a paddle and from the first bounce of the ball could play fairly well for a beginner.

Behind the lodge, a few picnic tables and benches marked the area for crafts and nature study. I was not particularly interested in studying nature, which as I remember consisted of learning the names of trees by looking at their leaves. I ignored the stories leaves could tell us, and this no doubt contributed to a severe case of poison ivy I contracted on a hike. Local remedies proved useless, and I had to be taken back to Marion, where Dr. Keith gave me a shot.

I approached the crafts assignments with some enthusiasm, based perhaps on the quality of work being turned out by other campers. But I soon discovered I was inept at even the most basic crafts, such as lanyard weaving and belt making. I covered for my lack of ability by adopting an attitude of disdain for all handiwork, when in fact I saw it as a personal failing.

A white building behind the lodge may have been used for storage or for sleeping quarters for camp directors—or both. Behind this building stretched a pasture that was used for outdoor sports: baseball, archery, foot races, and field events, such as the high jump.

The only other structural feature of the main camp I recall was the campfire circle, set between the flagpole and the lodge, at a slightly lower level than the parade ground. Here on some evenings we sat on stone seats and listened to ghost stories and sang songs. There was singing in the mess hall, too, and the only songs I remember were mordant refrains about death.

*Whenever you see a hearse go by*
*You wonder if you'll be the next to die.*
*They wrap you up in a dirty shirt*
*And stuff you under the sand and dirt.*
*The worms crawl in, the worms crawl out*
*And bugs play pinochle on your snout.*

An almost endless song about a lethal peanut began:

*Found a peanut, found a peanut, found a peanut*
*just now.*
*Just now I found a peanut, found a peanut just*
*now.*

*Cracked it open, cracked it open, cracked it open*
*just now.*
*Just now I cracked it open, cracked it open just*
*now.*

*Found a worm in it, found a worm in it, found a*
*worm in it just now.*
*Just now I found a worm in it, found a worm in*
*it just now.*

*Ate it anyway, ate it anyway, ate it anyway just*
*now.*
*Just now I ate it anyway, ate it anyway just now.*

In later stanzas, the subject of this song gets sick, sees a doctor, has an operation, dies, is buried, goes to heaven, gets rejected, goes to hell, somehow returns to earth, and, I think, finds a peanut.

A special mess hall ritual, accompanied by song, occurred at least once a week. Counselors selected a camper for what might appear to be ridicule, but was instead an expression of affection. They sang a short song which I've entirely forgotten, but its theme could be expressed as "he's a goofball." Once chosen, the honored camper stood and behaved in some pre-scribed and goofy manner as the song continued. Ev-eryone cheered and clapped. I wanted tremendously to be chosen as a goofball. On goofball night, when the ceremony began after supper, I grew nervous with an-ticipation; perhaps this time I would be chosen. But I was passed over week after week, year after year. My little brother was chosen once—he performed with a big smile as all the campers laughed and applauded because he was so little and cute.

MY BROTHER and I, and two of the Hamilton boys— Jim and Dick—occupied a somewhat privileged posi-tion at camp. (The oldest Hamilton boy, Doug, was a counselor). For one thing, we spent the entire summer at Wapsie Y. Few other boys were so fortunate. Our longevity meant that we knew the routine well, and could take full advantage of loopholes in the rules.

Our other benefit, which no other camper shared, was that our mothers were there, silently and distantly looking out for us. The camp director, Mr. Salisbury, with the agreement of our mothers, was determined to treat us no differently from other campers. We were to have the same opportunities, such as competing in the

Saturday sports events, and were to follow the same rules, such as taking rest periods after lunch.

One summer I made an illicit attempt to function as an assistant in the camp store when it opened briefly after lunch. I was supposed to return to my cabin for rest period, but instead I assigned myself the job of passing candy bars to the counselor in charge of the store once a camper had placed his order. The camper would come to the sales counter and place his order with my associate: He would ask for a Baby Ruth, say. I was up on the counter a few feet away, but hidden by latticework. Hearing the order, I picked up a Baby Ruth and slid it along the counter to my associate, who handed it to the customer. It was as if the candy bar had materialized from nowhere, and I thought it was a wonderful effect. Mr. Salisbury caught me at this and ordered me to my cabin where I was to write a letter to my parents. This seemed illogical, since my mother was present and my father visited every weekend, bringing Spike, our dog.

I cannot cite a single instance where my mother's presence worked to my benefit, but it must have done so, for I was always aware that I had an ace in the hole. The one intervention I remember her making in my camping life involved a plate of spaghetti and meatballs. I could not eat spaghetti or anything that spaghetti touched. To me, those long, squirmy, tangled tubes were worms. They crawled in my sight. The sauce over the worms was mucus, slime, fecal matter. Spaghetti was not just inedible; it was nauseating. (Noodles had the same effect, but elbow macaroni bathed in cheese could be eaten cautiously.)

My mother knew how I felt about spaghetti, which was surely a camp staple, and she had tolerated my phobia for years, but one summer, for reasons long forgotten, she issued an ultimatum. I could not leave the table in the mess hall until I had eaten some spaghetti. All the other campers departed. I sat alone in the hall on a bench. The spaghetti and all its secretions turned cold and congealed before me. I would not eat. My mother, having told me what I must do, went about her work. The earth moved in its orbit and I did not pick up a fork.

Then a fellow camper entered the mess hall and came to my table, sitting across from me. His presence meant that the rest period had ended. It soon would be time for the afternoon swim. My visitor was not a special friend, but a sympathizer. He had a solution. He reminded me that if I took just one bite of the festering pile on my tray I could go free. He explained that if I held my nose while eating a single strand of spaghetti I would not taste it. He himself had used this remedy more than once. I explained to him that it was not only the smell that offended me. I was near tears and incoherent with shame. My rescuer then said I should close my eyes while holding my nose and eat just one bite. I moved slowly to follow his instructions, selecting the smallest morsel. Not seeing, not smelling, not chewing, not tasting, I swallowed a wisp of cold spaghetti. Then I broke from the table and ran to sunlight.

WE WENT swimming twice a day, mid-morning and following the afternoon rest period. It was by far my favorite activity. I knew how to swim before going to camp, and there I quickly passed through the first three stages of competence established by the YMCA:

Minnow, Fish, and Flying Fish. I still have my Minnow badge, preserved in a scrapbook about camp I made as a grade school assignment. The ultimate stage was Shark, but I never reached it because it was impossible to perform all the required feats in the river's swimming area—swimming a given distance, for example, or mastering dives that could only be performed in a proper pool.

We reached the swimming area by a pathway that led upstream and downhill to a flat area along the river that served as a beach. It may have been a sandbar. Tall grasses obscured the river until we reached the swimming area, and it was always thrilling to turn the corner and see the water. It was an opaque brown, and no trick of light or weather could make it seem blue.

Two cables with buoys stretched across the river to mark the limits of the swimming area. A raft was attached to the upstream cable, and the water on the beach side was shallow enough that non-swimmers could reach the raft. The far side of the raft led to deeper water.

I do not remember the effects of the river's current; we must have learned to adjust. Surely the river bottom was muddy, but I don't remember it being so, and, whatever its consistency, it did not inhibit our enjoyment.

A decent swimmer could easily reach the far side of the river, but it was an unappealing destination: a steep bank covered by a tangle of fallen trees—we knew this to be a habitat for snakes. A few times when we were in the river, a snake swam toward us, its head up like a periscope, side-winding its body through the water in a series of graceful arcs; it could swim faster than it could crawl. Was it a water moccasin? We always thought so, and began to yell and splash water until the snake, overwhelmed by the uproar, made a sudden pivot and swiveled back toward its den.

On Saturdays, the last full day in the camp week, boys could compete in a wide range of sports—track and field, swimming, archery. One year, when I was nine years old and classed in the junior division, I completely dominated the swimming events, week after week winning blue ribbons (made of paper) in such events as floating, submarine swim, 50-yard swim, 50-yard backstroke, 100-yard swim, and 220-yard swim. (The swimming area itself was well short of 220 yards, and probably didn't extend to 100 yards, so we must have had to swim upstream laps.)

While I was notching all those wins, Dick Hamilton, a year or so older than I, was going undefeated in the age-group division just above mine. Mr. Salisbury was unhappy with this combined dominance by cooks' children who already had too many privileges, so he changed the age limits in the various divisions, moving me into the same category as Dick Hamilton. I knew I could not beat Dick Hamilton in anything, and I thought it would be a disgrace not to win. It seemed to me that not racing at all would be preferable to losing.

I went to see my father, who was at the camp as always on weekends, fishing with Mr. Hamilton. I found him at their favorite spot, a short distance downstream from the camp. I proposed to him that I not enter the swimming competitions this week, as I was perhaps not feeling as well as I might. My dad must have known this was coming, for he remained calm. He said that I had been competing in these events for a long time, that I should not stop now, but should enter the races and do my best. Dick Hamilton's name did not come up; his father stood nearby, observing silently. I was not persuaded that my father's advice was the best course, but I had no option. I swam hard against Dick Hamilton, and almost kept pace, but could not catch him. My days as a camp champion had ended.

From time to time heavy rains caused the Wapsie to flood. Silt ran thick in the water and the sandbar beach was swamped, but the camp itself, high on its bank, was not threatened. If the flood was heavy, swimming was cancelled, but moderately high and muddy water was not sufficient reason to stay away. We walked through puddles to reach the swimming area, then plunged into the murky river, adjusting to its greater depth and the heavier pull of its current.

When the river was high like this we often swam like Johnny Weissmuller, who played Tarzan in the movies, with our heads up and chins dragging in the water. When we got back to camp, we wore little brown beards of Wapsipinicon mud, and were delighted to be so adorned. My mother wondered how much Iowa dirt we had swallowed, but it seemed to cause no harm.

NOT EVERYONE loved camp. Each summer, one or two homesick boys tried to run away. They were usually stopped somewhere along the dirt road that led to camp. Others disappeared for longer periods, but usually ended up at the Hutchins house, which was visible from the campsite. Mrs. Hutchins phoned the camp and matters were settled.

Snipe hunters also found comfort at the Hutchins house. These boys had fallen victim to the classic con game, perpetrated, against camp rules, by callous counselors. Here an eager youth is offered the opportunity to join some older boys in one of their favorite nighttime activities: capturing the elusive nocturnal bird known as snipe. The boy is taken into the dark woods and handed a gunny sack. Hold this, he is told, and the rest of us will go into the woods and chase the snipes in your direction; when they come running past, throw the sack over them. The older boys then disappear, leaving the innocent rube holding the bag.

A near tragedy occurred one summer, and many campers who were there remember it. A large tree had fallen into the river roughly opposite the boat dock. For reasons unclear to us, the tree was seen as a potential threat, and had to be removed. We watched as two or three men clambered along the tree's trunk and branches, and we understood they were attaching dynamite to the tree and planned to blow it to smithereens.

A fairly large crowd of boys gathered on the hillside near the lodge to watch. We were not close to the water's edge, but well removed on high ground. I stood under an eave of the lodge. When the blast went off, it was huge. Chunks of the tree blew into the air and soared across the river, crashing through the trees in front of the lodge. I heard them landing on the roof of the lodge and my first reaction was to laugh in surprise; we had not expected the explosion to be so powerful. An instant later, I realized I was in danger. Just before turning to run into the lodge, I looked to my right and saw a boy staggering down the hillside, about to pitch forward, blood gushing from his head. I scurried to safety and did not see what happened after that.

We were somber at the evening meal. We learned that some counselors had risked their safety to rescue the injured boy, that he was taken to the hospital, and that he was going to be all right.

If I ever knew who those dynamiters were and what they thought they were doing and why they were so bad at it, I have long since forgotten.

SUNDAY WAS change-over day, when old campers left and new campers arrived. Counselors and camp directors were busy managing the transition and the cooks were preparing the ham supper traditionally served on this day. The result was unusual freedom for the handful of boys who were staying over.

My father came each weekend, bringing our little fox-terrier mutt, Spike. Dad and Mr. Hamilton liked to fish for catfish and bullheads from the riverbank a few hundred yards downstream from the camp. One night my father left his baited fishing pole outside the cabin. He heard a noise and went out with a flashlight. It revealed a rat that had taken the bait and was now hooked and pulling against the line, rattling the fishing rod. Stanley solved the problem by cutting the line, and the rat ran off, carrying hook, line, and sinker.

Sometimes on those freelance Sundays my brother and I joined our father and Mr. Hamilton at their fishing spot. After a while, we wandered off to see what we might discover outside the boundaries. I do not remember that anyone cautioned us not to go exploring; rather, I think our rambles were considered normal boyish behavior and as such were unpreventable. Spike was always up for adventure, and he came with us.

There was a cow pasture not far from the fishing spot, and on one of our excursions with a few other boys, we found cows in it. We decided to cut across the pasture. As town boys, we were not familiar with the ways of cows. (Farm boys were unlikely to become campers; they needed to stay home and work.) I don't think that anyone in our little party deliberately provoked the cows; perhaps someone made a false move. But cows have their reasons, and one came after us. I believe it was a cow, not a bull, but it had a small set of horns. It was white with brown patches. It was upset.

Some of the boys—there were no more than four or five of us—escaped on foot, but my little brother and I opted to climb a tree. We grappled our way up it before the cow could catch us. To our surprise, it lurked under the tree, waiting to see if we would fall out, I guess. Spike, a tiny thing compared to the cow, harried it, barking and running at it, then retreating when the cow lowered its head and started a charge. We were terribly afraid for Spike and yelled at him to run home. After a while, he did just that, and we hoped he was going for help in the fabled way that great dogs always did.

There we were, Pete and I, treed by an angry and determined cow. I hesitate to tell you what came next, but I have promised to report what I remember. We know that even though memories might be wrong, they can still harbor truth. So this is what happened: The cow tried to climb the tree. It reared up on its back legs and put its front hoofs on the trunk. But it got no higher than that and soon was back down on all fours. It will take billions of years before cows evolve the ability to climb trees and punish little boys.

Finally our nemesis ambled away. Pete and I bolted for the mess hall, eager to tell our mother and friends what had happened. We were relieved to see

Spike there. He offered his usual joyful greeting, but seemed free of any guilt for failing to bring help. It was as if the entire adventure had slipped his mind. The boys who escaped were similarly unimpressed; they thought our run for the tree had been a stupid move. When we told our mother about being chased up a tree by a cow, she was only mildly interested, distracted perhaps by the pressures of her job. She acted as if we were telling a fib or had experienced an event that happened all the time.

THERE WERE some wonderful boys at camp, including a set of triplets who did not look very much alike. But perhaps the most memorable was Snake Palmer. He was an Iowa boy like the rest of us, but there was something exotic about him. He was a free-thinker, possessed of a cheerful defiance and seemingly wise beyond his years, like a street kid from Naples. He had thick black hair and tawny skin, made all the more so because he disdained T-shirts and went about bare-chested as often as he could. He spent all or most of the summer at camp, and may have been a junior counselor. There is no photo of him in my scrapbook, but I see him clearly in my mind's eye, shirtless and smiling in the sun, wearing a bull snake around his neck like a scarf.

Snake Palmer loved snakes, and apparently they loved him too. On Sundays, he showed us where he got them. Farther downstream from where my father and Mr. Hamilton fished, a dead tree had fallen partway into the river. Its trunk hugged the river bank while its branches stretched far out over the water. On sunny days, the tree was a reptilian paradise. Turtles of various sizes lounged on the trunk and snakes hung from its branches like spaghetti from a fork. We called the place Snake Island, though there was no island involved. Snake's Tree, we should have called it.

Snake showed us how to sneak up on turtles, which for all their humped lassitude were wary. An indiscreet movement by one of us prompted a brief scramble from the turtles before they plopped safely into the river. Still, we caught some and brought them back to camp. We set them up in cardboard boxes, where they eventually perished, escaped, or were freed by a sympathetic passerby.

We left the snakes to Snake. He had them stashed in various places and often had one in his pocket or hand. Iowa has a few poisonous snakes, and I'm sure Snake Palmer knew who they were.

Snake's greatest moment came late in the camping season. He had collected a two-foot specimen that he kept in a cardboard box, topped by a screen, just outside the door of the cooks' cabin. (My mother was not afraid of snakes, nor, apparently, was Mrs. Hamilton.)

One day Snake's snake had babies. Tiny little snakes crawled out of her belly and wriggled furiously on the bottom of the box. We had never seen a birth of any kind, and watched this one with amazement. Not all snakes came out of eggs. These came out of bellies, alive and hungry.

I don't remember whether Snake Palmer was able to feed and raise those babies, but I feel certain he would have tried. After all, that's what good fathers do.

PERHAPS THE year Snake's snake had babies was also the year I began to learn a little something about the reproductive act among humans.

After eight weeks devoted to camp for boys, Wapsie Y was converted for a week or two to a bible camp for girls. My mother and Mrs. Hamilton stayed on to cook, and this meant that any boys still at camp had to vacate the cabins. One year Pete and I shared a tent with two of the Hamilton boys, Dick and Jim. The tent was pitched under a tree not far from the cooks' cabin. Jim, a muscular blond, was older than the rest of us and may have been a junior counselor.

As is natural under such living arrangements, the talk turned to the use of penises. This was not the only subject by any means, but it did come up. So far as I knew at the time, the penis had only one purpose. Jim, who may have gotten his information from his older brother, Doug, described another purpose, that of coupling with a female. I did not clearly understand how this act was accomplished, but I remember Jim explaining that it involved the penis getting bigger.

One morning on awakening, I thought my penis had achieved the state Jim described. I showed him the hairless little nub, slightly larger than normal. No, Jim said, this only means you have to take a pee. I was relieved to hear this, and I recall no further discussions along these lines.

In addition to occupying the cabins, the females at bible camp also took over the rooms in the latrine normally used by boys, and the few boys left at camp visited the much smaller room that had been used by females. The boys' section—now the girls'—consisted of two large rooms. The first room contained sinks, some toilets, and, against the west wall, a metal trough, roughly ten feet long, that boys used as a urinal. The urinal was flushed from a sprinkling pipe that ran along the top of the trough. We liked to joke that the girls used the urinal to wash their feet.

Beyond this room were the showers, an open room with perhaps six or eight shower heads.

The other section of the latrine, now used by boys, was the size of a small bathroom, containing a toilet, sink, and a shower. It backed up to the girls' shower room.

One day, some boys came to me with exciting news. There were holes in the wall between the boys' bathroom and the girls' shower. It was almost shower time for the girls. The girls who went to bible camp were older than the boys who went to camp, years older than I. The boys invited me to come and see what I could see. (I should say at this point that the boys in question were not the Hamilton brothers, nor was my brother, Pete, involved.)

We went to the latrine. The holes were bigger than I had imagined. Some girls were showering. The boys peeked through the holes, then offered one to me. I put my eye to the hole and peered into the steamy room. There they were, bare flanks and breasts, a sight I had never seen.

Then, walking toward me, I saw an older girl, a woman maybe, chunky in her nakedness, with heavy breasts and dark hair below her stomach. She seemed to be looking right at me, directly through the peephole into my exposed eyeball. Fear hit me like a charge of electricity.

Panic-stricken, I pulled back from the peephole and ran wildly from the latrine. I cut behind the mess hall, heading out of camp, as far away as I could get. I paused to take a breath and was surprised to see the other boys running after me.

Where are you going? they asked me when they caught up.

I had to get away, I said.

We thought you were going to tell on us.

I will never tell anyone, I said.

And, with one exception, I never have, until now.

AT TWILIGHT during boy's camp, we assembled to witness the lowering of the flag. Two boys worked the ropes to bring it down and then folded it into a tri-angle. It would be stored in the lodge until the next morning. We sang the first verse of "Taps."

*Day is done, gone the sun*
*From the lakes, from the hills, from the sky.*
*All is well, safely rest,*
*God is nigh.*

# VIII.

## ALL IN A DAY'S WORK

## *Read All About It*

NEWSPAPERING CAN be a tough racket. I discovered that when the paper I worked for decided to issue an extra.

I knew what an extra was: A special edition of the paper announcing a huge story, a news development so astounding it could not wait until the next day. I had seen them in the movies and comic books. Clark Kent's newspaper, the *Daily Planet*, issued extras. Billy Batson, the newsboy who turned into Captain Marvel by speaking the magic word "shazam," also shouted "Extra, extra, read all about it" to bustling city crowds when he wasn't administering justice as a super hero.

Now my paper was planning an extra. This was in 1948, before television rendered the practice nearly obsolete. I was about twelve, one of perhaps twenty boys who delivered the *Cedar Rapids Gazette* to customers in Marion.

I learned about the extra from Chuck Kent, a boy whose work ethic was legendary. Not only was he the top *Gazette* carrier in Marion, but he also worked in a gas station and was accumulating merit badges at a torrid pace on his way to becoming an Eagle Scout.

Chuck had been chosen by the *Gazette* to sell copies of the extra on the streets of Marion's business district, and Chuck picked me to be his assistant. We would be just like the newsboys of fiction and movies, hawking newspapers about the most sensational local story in years.

The story involved a death in a hotel room. A young man and woman had met there. Things happened, things never completely disclosed in the newspaper accounts, and the woman died. The young man was charged with murder. He claimed it was an accident. The trial had gone on for days, provoking large headlines, long stories, and much gossip.

Now the case had gone to the jury. A verdict was expected that afternoon. The *Gazette* was an evening paper, so Chuck and I were instructed to make our deliveries of the regular edition, then report back to the Marion office of the paper and await the arrival of the extra.

Chuck may have remained calm, but I was excited, not because of the impending news, but because I wanted to see what an extra looked like; I wanted to examine this rare journalistic specimen.

When Chuck and I met, the newspaper office was closed. We waited in the doorway as dusk settled over the town. The stores began closing: Kendall's Hardware, the Danish Made Bakery, Edison's Drug Store. The street lights, strung on wires over Main Street, came on. Then the last store went dark as Mike Cira turned off the lights in his grocery store and soda fountain.

It was nearly nine o'clock when the *Gazette* truck arrived and someone threw off our small bundle of extras. We snipped the wire and pulled out the paper, still warm and smelling of wet ink.

The headlines screamed that the jury had declared the boy not guilty, but I wanted to know what the extra looked like inside. I envisioned a whole new paper. I turned the front page and was shocked to see that the contents were exactly the same as those of the papers we had delivered hours earlier. The comics, the sports section, the picture page—I had already read them, and so had hundreds of other people living in Marion.

As I began to doubt the viability of our project, Chuck and I divided up the papers and started looking for buyers. Uptown was nearly deserted. We would be yelling "Extra!" to empty streets. We offered our papers quietly and unsuccessfully to a few stragglers.

When the movie let out around ten o'clock, we accosted the small group of citizens who trickled onto the sidewalk. They had not heard the news of the verdict. A few forked over a nickel to buy a paper, but most escaped.

Then we were alone again. The neon lights flickered in the windows of Ping's Scoreboard, the largest beer tavern in town. Neither of us had ever been in a tavern before, but Chuck's business instincts took over.

We can sell papers in there, he argued. Let's go in. It's our only chance. I had been trained to avoid taverns. I could not bring myself to join him.

As Chuck disappeared through the Scoreboard's doors I began to walk slowly home, a distance of about half a mile. No one was on Main Street. When I got out of the business district, walking past homes where lights still shone, I began softly calling, Extra, extra. I did not want to alarm anyone.

There was no reaction until I was about a block from home. A man in his undershirt came out his front door. A customer, I thought.

What are you doing? he asked.

Selling extras, I said, lifting up the bundle of papers under my arm.

Be quiet, he said. Go home.

And so I did.

The next day, Chuck told me he had sold a dozen papers. I had a few nickels in my pocket and about fifteen newspapers that were truly extra.

## Tough Route Seven

BECOMING A paperboy was a common early step in the hierarchy of jobs that boys held as they matured through high school. My own career track included working as a baby sitter, paperboy, mower of grass, shoveler of snow, usher at the movies, and supermarket carryout boy.

Boys and girls were expected to work from an early age, and there was no shortage of opportunities. Many retailers offered part-time jobs to youngsters, juggling work schedules to fit the kids' school obligations. Employing youngsters was practically a civic duty. Child labor was cheap labor, to be sure, but the greater purpose was to teach young people that work was precious and doing it well was an essential life skill. This was the lesson the Depression had so cruelly taught our parents, and they passed it on to their children.

The first step to becoming a *Cedar Rapids Gazette* paperboy was to serve as a "sub"—a substitute, or assistant, to the boy who managed the route. Subs worked alongside their bosses, although they might not be needed on days the paper was light, such as Saturdays. They were expected to know the route well enough to take it over when their superior was grounded by the flu.

Subs didn't last long. Those unmotivated by the work sought jobs elsewhere; the good ones soon graduated to a route of their own.

I became a paperboy at the age of ten or eleven, but I didn't just deliver the paper—I also read it. The *Gazette* offered national and local news in greater depth and variety than the radio—and better yet, it had pictures, ink-heavy and blurred though they were. The *Gazette's* photos had nowhere near the clarity of those in *Life* magazine, but they were available every day, and once in a while someone you knew was in one of them.

The front page was invariably topped by an eight-column headline in all capital letters. Each day, that headline said, something very important had happened. Sometimes it was an international event, sometimes a local tragedy, such as the death of a boy who was struck by a batted baseball, sometimes the score of a World Series game, played in the East that afternoon and completed in time for a wrap-up to appear in the evening *Gazette*. As many as fifteen stories were jammed on page one, offering news, features, and oddities, with just enough room left over for a contents box and "Today's Chuckle." (For example, "A will stipulated that everything was to be left to the deceased's wife, provided she married again within a year. He wanted someone to be sorry he died.")

The back page was the picture page, and that's where I started reading, scanning the photos of car wrecks, boxing matches, people in the news, and sometimes a bit of modest cheesecake, all rendered in heavy black ink. "Ripley's Believe it or Not!" reliably filled the lower right hand corner. It was a two-column box with sketches illustrating wonders from around the world. ("A gorilla never sleeps twice in the same place." "A dog in Pennsylvania crows like a rooster!")

Then I flipped forward, pausing to read the comics, tracking the predicaments of Li'l Abner, Joe Palooka, Steve Canyon, and others. Forward then, to the news from the entertainment world. I read the brief movie reviews by Nadine Subotnik and scrutinized the movie ads, memorizing the stars of each film. I studied Walter Winchell's column from New York, looking for clues to life on the Great White Way. Many of the names were unfamiliar, but New York called to me: So much happened there.

Now I flipped to the sports section, which took most of my reading time. I paid no attention to farm news, the women's pages, and most local doings. I often read while lying on the floor of the living room, inhaling the pulpy, inky smell of the paper as I absorbed its messages. Sometimes my little brother lay on my back, and I could share my views on the day's events.

So, when I gathered with my fellow paperboys in the *Gazette's* Marion office on Tenth Street opposite the Marion Theatre, I was more interested than most in what was actually in the paper. I felt the romance of journalism.

Some two dozen boys assembled each evening, Monday through Saturday, and on Sunday mornings, in the main room of the small building. There were two other rooms, one of which was for the paper's Marion correspondent, who never seemed to be there. The other room was occupied by a woman whose duties were not clear to me. Perhaps she sold advertising and gathered the personal items that dotted the Marion

News column. ("Mrs. C___ J___ , of Marengo, was visiting the home of her cousin in Marion, Mrs. B___ J___, of___ 10th Ave., when she was called back home due to the death of her father.")

When the papers came in, they were heaved in bundles from a truck to the sidewalk in front of the office, and we surged out to find our bundle, then lugged it back inside to cut the wire and begin folding the papers. There was barely room to work. We sat on the floor or crowded onto benches that lined two sides of the room.

We folded almost every paper—perhaps sixty or seventy per route—and stuck it in a bag. Folding was an essential craft, for most of the papers would be hurled fifteen or twenty feet from the sidewalk to a porch, often while our bikes were in motion, and we did not want them to come apart in the air. On Mondays through Fridays, when the papers ranged from twenty to forty pages in size, we folded them into a scroll-like shape. We tossed them with an overhand motion, as if throwing a German stick hand grenade, or a hatchet.

The Saturday paper was only twelve pages. We folded it into a square and scaled it backhand, as we would later toss a Frisbee, so that it fluttered in a wobbly arc to the porch. I do not recall ever hearing a customer complain that his enjoyment of the paper was lessened because of the extra creases we had applied. On Sunday mornings the paper was too big to fold, so we doubled it over and secured it with a rubber band.

Paper folding was grimy work. The ink was still wet, and even when dry it easily rubbed off on anything that touched it. So each evening our hands and shirts became sooty, and our canvas bags were as filthy as a coal miner's handkerchief.

Presiding over this gaggle of boys was a rotund man seated at a roll-top desk. His name was Fred Ross. He wore a wrinkled dress shirt with sleeves rolled up and a threadbare tie, but no jacket. His beltless pants were held up by suspenders that stretched over his belly. He wore wool trousers and high-top shoes, and his job was to manage subscriptions in Marion and oversee the delivery crew. He ignored us as much as possible as we assembled our loads.

Fred Ross always had the wet butt of an unlit cigar in his mouth. He had smoked it during the day, and by the time we arrived at the office, there was only stub enough left for him to chew. Now, in late afternoon, a malodorous haze filled the room. The smell of Fred Ross's cigar, that is, the gag-inducing stink of something distinctly dead and rotting, was the dominant odor, but it mixed with the bitter smell of wet ink, the woody scent of damp paper, and the mingled stench that rose from the jumble of our two-dozen bodies— sweat and dust in the summer, mud in the spring, wet flannel on snowy days. Folding papers was a memorably fragrant experience. It was part of the romance of journalism.

Early in my career I became aware of a boy whose name I remember as Jim Tallman, an older boy who was an incredibly fast folder. He did it almost unconsciously, talking to others as his hands flew in their task, whisking the papers together at a blistering rate. I set out to match him. After a time, I was able to fold as many as five or ten papers in a row at the same velocity as Tallman, but I could not sustain the pace through the whole pile of papers.

We sought speed and efficiency in all our actions, for our goal was not so much to be productive as it was to spend as little time as possible on this matter of delivering papers. Once our route was completed there were other, more important things to do, such as shooting baskets, listening to our favorite radio shows, hunting rabbits, or reading comic books. We resented the precious seconds it took to serve a customer who insisted that we climb her steps and place the paper inside her storm door.

The papers folded, we hung our canvas bags over the handles of our bicycles and spun off on our routes. Jim Tallman had what I considered the best route in the city, Number Twelve, almost a straight shot down Twelfth Street. He and a sub, each taking one side of the street, could finish in a matter of minutes.

I would later inherit Tallman's route, but for now I had to face Route Seven, the worst in the system. The route began at the edge of the business district and ran out east to the very end of town. It was long, it had fewer customers than most, and it was complicated. The first stop was an apartment complex on the south side of Main Street next to Chesley's Club Royale, a beer tavern. The tavern's doors were left open on summer afternoons to air out the place. The smell of stale beer, cigarette smoke, and wet sawdust poured into the street.

The apartment building could not have been more than two stories high, but I remember it as a cliff dwelling. I had to climb to the top to deliver a single paper. The wooden stairs clung to the side of the building like a fire escape. It did not feel right, in the middle of Iowa, to climb steps leading to someone's home, passing doorways to other people's homes. It was as if they all lived in a motel. There was a smell of boiled cabbage.

This was a long haul to dispense a single paper; I was not disappointed when the customer stopped his subscription. Ahead of me lay Seventh Avenue and a maze of side streets. Seventh Avenue was both Main Street and the highway through town. If I had a sub, he could take one side of the street and I the other. But my subs soon quit, for this was an unrewarding route when measured by time spent delivering each paper. They could make more money faster on other routes, and perhaps find a better boss.

With no sub, I had to crisscross the highway for about eight blocks, dodging traffic and mounting curbs. It was often more efficient, especially in winter, to walk the route rather than ride a bike. At about Twentieth Street, I had to tack north and cover part of Eighth Avenue until it expired in a corn field. There were some exasperating side streets, one of which held a single customer in the very last house, behind a gate. If I was on a bike, I had to dismount and open the gate before tossing the paper. If I was afoot, the roundtrip, amounting to two blocks, was, according to a newsboy's time value of money, punishingly unprofitable.

On Sunday mornings in bad weather, my father sometimes helped me deliver papers from his car. This was a rarity. I often came home soaked or chilled or both.

There were many dogs. I made friends, or at least established peaceful relations, with most, including a boxer on Twenty-First Street that was leashed to a clothesline. The dog, understanding it could not attack me if I kept my distance, simply ignored me. I was a fan of boxing and here was a dog called a boxer. I thought he was beautiful, but I gave him his space.

Another dog, guarding a small house on Eighth Avenue, wanted to kill me. He was not a huge dog, slightly smaller than the boxer, but dark, muscular, and evil tempered. His body was shaped like a torpedo, his head like a gargoyle. I dreaded approaching his house, hoping he would be inside, and he often was. Sometimes I found him chained up on the front porch. He did not bark when I appeared, but began a low growl, showing his teeth. He was too smart to lunge against his chain. I pitched the paper onto his porch and moved on. I swear I never taunted him, except in my mind. Sometimes he appeared, unchained, from behind the house, but not before I had delivered the paper and moved out of his territory. That was always my plan: to approach with stealth and depart in haste.

Then the inevitable: One dark winter night I heard a low cough from the shadows of the porch and the dog came at me like a bullet. I whirled in panic and ran across the street, hoping to climb something. I could hear him behind me; I expected to be dragged down. When I reached the house across the street, I turned to face my attacker, but he had disappeared.

That night I confessed to my father how frightened I was. He called the owner of the dog and arranged a meeting. We went to the owner's house. I sat in the living room on a couch. The dog was brought in. We looked at each other. The dog pretended not to recognize me. He was encouraged to sniff my hand. He did so, but we both knew it meant nothing. I did not attempt to pet him. There was no truce.

I never saw the dog again. I'm not sure why. Perhaps he was kept inside. Or this may have been when I induced Wally DeWoody to be my sub. I assigned him the back half of the route, since he lived in that neighborhood. The appeal was that when his papers were gone, he would be close to home—providing, of course, he could avoid being eaten. Or perhaps that was when I was transferred to Tallman's superb Route Twelve.

A block or two from DeWoody's house lay the last settlement in town. At least that's the way I perceived it, a sort of frontier village. Here sat a short row of tiny homes, no more than shacks, and a trailer or two. A few of them took the paper. Across the street from this settlement, cornfields spread endlessly under a vast sky. It was only a poor neighborhood on the outskirts of town, but when I picture myself there as an eleven-year-old, it is always cold, dark, and lonely, swept by strong winds with a storm brewing. Here civilization ended and eternity began.

One day I neared the end of the route with an urgent need to urinate. There was a diner not far away, but I was too shy to use its bathroom. I did not want to be seen relieving myself in the street. So I tried to hold it until I got home. I failed. Everything gave way and the front of my jeans was soaked down to the kneecaps.

I covered myself with my canvas bag and finished my route. At home, there was no hiding what had happened. I sat in a chair in the kitchen as my father talked to me. He was not angry.

Did you go before you left school? he asked.

I forgot.

Why didn't you go to the diner?

I don't know.

He offered some advice.

Danny, just go behind a tree.

With my father's permission, I have used this remedy most satisfactorily ever since.

## *Payday*

"MAY I collect?" This was the sound of Saturday morning in Marion, as its paperboys called on their customers for payment for the *Cedar Rapids Gazette* delivered on each of the prior seven days.

It made for a long morning, but here was the paperboy's reward for his week's work. To handle the collection process efficiently, most of us acquired (often from a retiring paperboy) a train conductor's change machine that we hooked to our belts. We carried a hand punch to put a distinctive hole in the *Gazette* subscriber card our customers handed us along with some coins or a dollar bill. The punch was their receipt for payment. We could recognize the shape of our punch and would be alerted if anyone punched his own card and tried to claim he had already paid. Of course no one ever attempted such a forgery.

I am not certain what the weekly subscription rate was. The newsstand price of the *Gazette* was five cents for Monday through Saturday, and ten cents for Sunday. Let's say the delivery price was thirty-five cents a week.

"May I collect?" we asked each of our fifty to seventy customers. And in almost every case, we did collect. The customers may not have felt any gratitude to the corporate institution of the *Cedar Rapids Gazette,* but even those most strapped for cash had no desire to stiff an eleven-year-old. Only a few failed to answer our knocks on any given Saturday. (Chuck Kent devised a way to flush out the slow payers. He deliberately "missed" their next paper. When they called for it, he delivered it promptly and collected what was owed.)

Paperboys worked at an age and for wages that might violate labor laws today, but they surely contributed to the *Gazette's* success. They were a low-cost distribution system that provided a reliable income stream. And they afforded a way for thrifty subscribers to pay as they read, in small weekly amounts, rather than have to come up with the cost of a whole year's subscription in advance. (A few customers did pay annually and by mail. We called them "regulars," and gratefully passed them by on collection day.)

Despite the low pay and daily demands of the job, I felt a dim pride in being part of the organization. I was interested in what the newspaper had to say. I read it, or parts of it, every day. I sensed a certain romance in journalism, and it touched me, even on the lowest rung of the ladder.

In addition to delivering the paper, The *Gazette* found other uses for its paperboys. It created a contest that rewarded those who could sign the most new subscriptions (we did not normally think of this as part of the job). The grand prize might be a new bicycle, while runners-up received tickets to an Iowa football game.

The newspaper also used its paperboy network to survey customers. The *Gazette* wanted to know what its subscribers thought about certain business issues. In my time, the paper owned a radio station, KCRG, which broadcast on an AM frequency. It was considering starting an FM affiliate, and needed to know if people in the listening area would be interested. This was an important matter because customers who wanted to hear KCRG-FM might have to buy a new radio with the capacity to receive FM. Some folks still had big wooden radios in their front rooms and these might become obsolete in an FM world.

The *Gazette* asked its paperboys to help measure the consumer mood on this subject. We were provided a little green card to fill out for each customer surveyed. As I recall, the answers were either yes or no; it couldn't have been very complicated.

I don't remember whether we were paid for this effort, and I would not like to make false accusations, so I will say, without fear of inaccuracy, that if we were paid anything at all, it wasn't much.

The survey, however, was flawed. Customers didn't know what FM was, and neither did I. The card coached us to explain that FM radio had less static than AM, but this did not seem to arouse much excitement. The card also provided a definition of FM.

When I asked my customers if they wanted FM radio, the conversation often went like this:

Well, I don't know, young man, what does FM mean?

It means frequency modulation.

There was a moment of silence as my customer pondered this information.

Well, I guess I can't rightly say I'm for it.

Based on my survey, I thought the *Gazette* would be extremely foolish to go into the FM radio business, but it did so anyway and made a success of it. Television came along a few years later, and the company got into that right away, too, and probably didn't require a survey before making the move.

It took most of the morning to collect for the whole route. A sixty-paper route would result in a collection of about twenty-one dollars, probably a little less when absentees and regulars were deducted.

We then reported to the *Gazette* office and presented our money, mostly in coins, to Fred Ross, a short, round man who was in charge of circulation in Marion. Seated at his roll-top desk and chewing his dead cigar, Fred Ross counted every penny, gave us credit for the few regulars who paid by the year, and made the necessary adjustments for customers who had not paid that day. I am not sure how this worked, but I can say for the *Gazette* that its paperboys were not required to bear the total cost of delinquent customers. Instead, that liability was shared until the customer made up the arrears.

What did we earn? Memory says it was ten cents per customer, or six dollars on a sixty-paper route. For this we had worked at least an hour every day delivering papers and at least two hours collecting. That works out to sixty-six cents an hour. But wait a minute. We had to pay our subs, the boys who assisted us in delivering the paper. A fair distribution to a full-time sub might be two dollars, since he did not have to collect.

What would two dollars mean to a sub? Wally DeWoody remembered years later that the money I had paid him would buy the following: admission to the movies, a box of .22-caliber shells, a bottle of soda pop, and a snow cone.

This sounds like less than two dollars, and De-Woody's expression told me he felt he had been grossly underpaid. Well, as I've said before, newspapering is a tough racket. You have to feel the romance of it.

## *Night Moves*

THE SUMMER I turned thirteen, I went into show business, working as an usher at the Marion Theatre. In those last days before the onslaught of television, the movie house was one of the most important cultural centers in town, along with the school system, the churches, and the library, so it was to me something of a privilege to work there. Certainly the pay was no attraction.

I was hired through the intercession of my best friend, Tom Domer. He was the same age as I but had a far more important job at the theater. He ran the refreshment stand, popping up a flood of big yellow kernels in hot oil and selling Milk Duds, Junior Mints, and Chuckles. Soft drinks were not allowed. Tom's stand was a three-tiered glass case about the length of an office work station.

Tom's job also required him, three times a week, to climb a ladder and hang the metal letters on the marquee that announced the latest double feature. I stood below, handing the letters up to him, helping with the spelling and spacing.

We also changed the promotional material in the glass cases that flanked the ticket booth. The left case held the colorful poster that heralded the main feature. The right case held the poster for the second feature. Around each poster Tom put glossy black-and-white photographs that purported to show scenes from the movie. All this material came packaged with the reels of film to be shown. In time, I realized that some of the black-and-white images did not appear in the movie itself. I considered these inconsistencies a minor betrayal on the part of Hollywood, false advertising, I guess. I took pride in identifying the fake photos and bringing them to the attention of my friends. Since I had no explanation for the forgeries, my friends quickly lost interest in them. I continued my inquiries, wondering what Hollywood was up to.

The theater's auditorium had two aisles downstairs with rows of perhaps four or six seats outside each aisle and eight or ten seats in the center. Twisting stairs on the right side of the lobby led to a small balcony. The projection room sat behind and above the balcony. Tom, whose career at the theater was longer than mine, eventually learned to run the projector, occasionally filling in when the regular operator was away. Tom was only thirteen or fourteen when he performed this duty. He wasn't needed often. The regular projectionist was typically prompt for every matinee and evening show, climbing to the balcony and disappearing, hermit-like, into his small black den. He slept in a rented room above a nearby store, and folks hardly ever saw him on the street.

I was assigned to be the usher on the aisle on the right. A female classmate handled the left aisle. As is often the case in the lower rungs of the entertainment industry, the pay was appalling. I received twenty cents a night. I was also entitled to a box of popcorn, but only if enough was left over after the last customer was served. (Tom planned it so that was always the case.) Another benefit, we were told, was that the ushers could watch the movies when we weren't busy seating people. This was a paltry advantage, though, because the balcony overhang blocked out the top of the screen. We had to crouch down or bend over to get the full picture. So our remuneration was twenty cents in cash and ten cents in popcorn valued at retail. The deal was supposedly sweetened by the thirty-five cents we didn't have to pay to get into the place. For this we worked three hours.

When I reported for duty that first night, I received no training. I was handed a flashlight and shown my post. The lights went off and the movie started. People came in and stood at the top of the aisle waiting for their eyes to adjust. I didn't know how to address them. I appeared out of the blackness and said something like, Would you like to be ushered? They looked down at me as if I had made a rude suggestion and pushed past me into the dark. Then Tom recommended I say, Hello, may I help you? Where would you like to sit? After that, things went much better.

The Marion Theatre, strictly a second-run house, showed double features every night with matinees on Saturdays and Sundays. Evening admission prices were fifteen cents for children under twelve and thirty-five cents for older children and adults. Matinees cost a dime for children under twelve and a quarter for everyone else.

As I recall, a new double feature was shown three times a week, with the cycle being Sunday-Monday, Tuesday-Wednesday-Thursday, and Friday-Saturday. Ushers were not required for every showing, only for those when larger crowds were expected. Movies with Ma and Pa Kettle, Tom remembered, filled the theater. Younger audiences split a gut on the antics of a young comedy duo, Dean Martin and Jerry Lewis.

Wednesday was Bank Night, when drawings were held for real money—$25, $50, even more. The lights came up and Gilbert Rathman, the theater manager, wheeled out a glass-sided case that was three-quarters full of paper slips. He thrust his hand into the case, stirred it around and pulled out a slip. Then he read off the name. The chosen had to be present to win, and that summer none were.

The evening show began at 7:00. First came previews, a newsreel, and selected short subjects, followed by the main feature. Then the second feature was shown. After that came a second showing of the shorts and the main feature. Shortly after the main feature began the second time, the ushers went off duty. By then, it was about 10:00 p.m. The refreshment stand closed about a half-hour later. Sometimes I stayed to watch the movie again. While I munched my free popcorn, smitten by Claudette Colbert in a black turtleneck sweater, Tom was in the balcony, smooching with the female usher. She taught me a lot, Tom confessed much later.

You may wonder why ushers were needed. We don't have them today. But in those days, people paid little attention to movie starting times, even though they were posted in the paper. Moviegoers came in when they felt like it, the movie well underway and the house dark as pitch. They needed help finding a seat.

Once seated, they watched the movie in progress, enjoyed the second feature, absorbed the short subjects, then watched the first movie again until someone in the group said, This is where we came in. So they stood up, stumbled to the aisle, bumping the knees of those still watching, and left the theater, where, once outside, visions of Hollywood dissolved in the steamy summer air.

Alfred Hitchcock, it is said, changed all that with *Psycho*, which came out in 1960. Daringly, Hitchcock insisted that no one be seated after the movie started. It was a revolutionary idea that theater managers at first resisted. But the movie was so powerful that they fell in line. The idea caught on and it soon became common practice for folks to see movies from the beginning. Meanwhile, the practice of showing double features faded away. That's why you seldom see thirteen-year-old ushers anymore.

# IX.

# GROWING INTO SPORTS

## *Inheritance*

THE OLD man is lying on his back in the living room, looking up at the four-year-old boy.

Ooh, groans the old man. What hit me?

The little boy is silent, smiling as he looks down on the man.

Was it a train?

The boy shakes his head no.

Was it a bus?

The boy shakes his head no.

Was it a . . . bear?

No, no, no. The boy's smile widens.

Well, then, was it . . . you?

The boy nods and laughs. The man pulls himself into a seated position.

You hit like a ton of bricks, the man groans.

The boy scampers back across the room, turns and rushes forward, throwing himself against the man's chest. The man catches the boy in his arms. Ooof, he says. He falls on his back and releases the boy, who jumps to his feet, smiling.

Ooh, the man groans, what hit me?

THIS IS my only memory of my grandfather, Roy, Stanley's father. My middle name is Roy. He died when I was very young. He was, according to an article in the *Marion Sentinel* in 1939, a sports fan who had been an athlete in his youth.

Roy was born April 20, 1877, on a farm twelve miles from Hutchinson, Kansas, a year after his family moved from Indiana in search of cheap land. He was one of eight children. According to the *Sentinel*, the family "proved up on one of Uncle Sam's timber claims," which apparently meant the family acquired farmland through the Homestead Act under terms that included the requirement to plant "ten acres of trees. They were cottonwoods."

Then the wheat crop failed, "and sometimes there was little else than corn bread, molasses, and home-made hominy." Roy went to rural schools and was tutored by his mother, who had taught school in Indiana. I inherited his report cards. He received excellent grades, scoring in the 90s in almost all his classes, the equivalent, I imagine, of getting straight As.

I have a photograph of Roy and four brothers, taken, I think, when Roy was in his forties. The brothers are wearing white shirts and ties and dark trousers. Instead of standing and facing the camera, they are all hunkered down in a squat. Roy is in the center, flanked on his right by Lester and Rupert, and on his left by Ed and Walter.

Why did they choose this crouching pose? I think I know. When the photo was taken, the brothers had grown up and set off on their own careers. They lived far apart. In the photo they are dressed up and wearing neckties, so they must have gathered at a reunion of some kind. They rarely saw one another. When someone volunteered to take a photo of all the boys together, Roy, something of a wit, said to his brothers, Let's show them what we learned in Kansas. So they all squatted down, resting on the strength of their thighs, the way farmers back home did it, taking a break from their chores to think things over for a few minutes before spitting in the dirt and getting back to work.

(The *Sentinel* story mentioned earlier said that Roy was one of eight children. In his later obituary, the listed survivors include the four brothers but no other siblings. Apparently three were lost at an early age.)

At the age of twenty-two, Roy left the farm in Kansas to attend telegraphy school in Wisconsin. He worked as a telegrapher in several towns, including Mason City, Iowa, where he met and married Cleora Hill in 1901. Cleora was a spirited girl, barely five feet tall. Roy's letters to her begin, "My dear little girlie." She called him "Kansas Calamity."

Their sons, Lester and Stanley, were born in Mason City. A few years later Roy became a mail clerk, working out of Marion, and stayed in that job until after World War I. He then spent a decade selling insurance before "learning that he was not born to that art," the *Sentinel* said.

In 1931, the Depression in full force, he started the K-V Café in Marion. He worked long hours seven days a week to create "a wholesome and reliable eating place" with "the good steady business the establishment now enjoys," the *Sentinel* wrote.

Roy was nearly six feet tall, thin, and bald at an early age. The blurry photo in the *Sentinel* shows a man looking older than the sixty-two he was at the time.

"He has little time for sports, in which he gets some pleasure by remote control [the radio, presumably]. In his youth he played baseball and now reads the sport and other columns of his daily papers.

"In his younger days he might have been seen most any summer day beating it for the creek with a group of boys at his heels, with his promise out to teach them to swim. He would do that again if there was time. He believes he would like golf, but never tried it.

"He enjoys his contact with the public, and says he is thoroughly convinced that the mass of people are square and mean well, and they have made him little trouble.

"He says he has no time for hobbies, but his wife admits he has one. His grandson."

ROY MUST have been proud of his sons' athletic accomplishments. Lester, the older, was quarterback on the high school football team and a guard in basketball. Stanley was a basketball star despite his twice-broken left arm, which he could not straighten. He was Marion's high scorer in both his junior and senior years, a standout on teams that finished a combined 17–21. In one game, a loss to the Coe College freshmen, Marion scored only eleven points and Stanley made eight of them, "the Marion ace slipping through the Crimson guards for four field goals," the paper reported. He later played for Cornell College, at least as a freshman, and perhaps into his later years as well.

In his twenties, Stanley several times won the singles table tennis championship of Marion, then went on to regional contests in Cedar Rapids and other towns. He won no championships there, but advanced at least twice to the semi-finals. He later taught me some of the intricacies of the game. I was never really able to beat him. As I improved, he sometimes let me win, I think, by restricting his own game in some way, such as refusing easy kill shots. These were hollow victories. Stanley played what might be called an all-court game, based more on finesse and strategy than power.

Stanley never talked about his athletic accomplishments. I knew nothing of his table tennis career. He talked about playing basketball only when asked, and then tended to make a joke out of it, laughing as he told us what I took to be an exaggeration.

When Pete and I were very young, we often stared at his broken arm. The left elbow was a large knot, as if a pointed kneecap had been implanted on the outside of his arm. We asked him if it hurt. Stanley said it didn't. We sometimes asked permission to touch it and he said okay. The skin was cool, with hard bone right underneath. How he broke it the first time is lost to memory; perhaps in a fall from his high chair, or from a tree. The second break came when he misjudged the depth of a swimming hole before diving into Indian Creek.

After a while, Pete and I forgot the strange broken elbow was there. It was just part of our dad and we never saw it as a handicap or a disfigurement.

MY GRANDFATHER died on April 28, 1943, eight days after his sixty-sixth birthday. I was six. My dad either met me outside or took me there to tell me. We stood near the side door, in the driveway. For some reason I thought it was best not to cry, and so I did not. I told myself I would cry later, in the bedroom when I was alone. When that time came I sat on the edge of my bed and tried to cry, but I wasn't able to do it.

## *Home Field Advantage*

WE GREW into sports. Our games and the ways we played them were handed down to us like well-worn clothes from older boys. Our inspiration came from high school athletes and the men who played in the town's softball league. With the end of World War II, a minor league baseball franchise was restored to Cedar Rapids, allowing us to study the moves and postures of real professionals, even though they played for a losing team.

In 1945 a tough new coach named Les Hipple took over the Marion High School teams and began turning out champions. Sports mania swept through the youthful population in town, and I was caught up in it.

No adults taught us how to hold a bat or punt a football. We learned from other players. No adults—except one, a mentally handicapped visionary—attempted to structure teams, organize games, or manage leagues. Some fathers played catch with their sons, or hit them flies and grounders—mine did—but when it came time to mount a game we were on our own.

Because we were small and playing fields were few, we pursued many of our sports in miniature. It took four boys to play football, but only two for baseball or basketball. We played in backyards, vacant lots, and driveways. Our house and yard became a four-season sports complex where we played those games and many more, including boxing, wrestling, golf, table tennis, skiing, and sledding. We even tried to create an ice-skating rink, but that didn't work out.

Our parents either supported (our father, almost always) or tolerated (our mother, uncomplainingly) all these efforts. They were not grooming future stars; they were letting boys be boys.

WHEN I was in fifth grade, Stanley responded to my requests for a basketball court. We nailed an orange hoop to the garage at the meticulously measured height of ten feet. I remember standing nearby and insisting on accuracy. Stanley hired a carpenter to construct a roughly triangular wooden backboard that just fit the peak of the garage front. Basketball backboards were going up all over town, and every one of them was homemade of wood. Either metal backboards for home use did not exist or they were outrageously expensive. Glass backboards were largely restricted to college gyms.

Stanley hung a powerful work light near the basket. It was attached to a long extension cord that snaked through a window into the bedroom Pete and I shared. Our driveway was one of the few places in town where basketball could be played after dark.

The driveway served a one-car garage and was thus very narrow. We played basketball there in all seasons, although we often had to chase balls that bounced out of bounds and rolled down a small slope to the left of the driveway. In winter, when the slope was covered in snow, the balls came back soaked. We had to towel them dry before resuming play. One winter day, inspired perhaps by Tom Sawyer's success in getting others to paint his fence, we tried to persuade my brother what a privilege it would be—and how much fun—for him to retrieve the balls and dry them for us while we played on with a spare ball. Pete, eager to please, gave it a try. Despite our praise, he soon realized he was being taken for a dupe and walked away in disgust. He knew he wasn't going to get into the game.

ONE YEAR, Pete and I asked our parents for skis. We thought we could schuss down the slope somewhat in the manner of the basketballs, hang a right and glide through the backyard of our neighbor, with no limits after that. We received the skis for Christmas, rudimentary black boards with a single leather strap over the toe for a binding. We could not get down that slope without exploding out of our bindings at the sudden flattening of the land, but it was not for the lack of trying. After a winter of awkward spills, we forsook our alpine dreams and retired the skis to the back of the garage.

Eighteenth Street, which ran downhill in front of our house, was one of the best sledding places in Marion. It was at the edge of town in those days, and saw little traffic. The street was not regularly plowed or cindered. With the first snowfall, we pulled our Flexible Fliers out of the garage and scoured the rust off their runners. Sometimes we used sandpaper; other times we simply scraped the runners on the driveway, marking the concrete with orange streaks.

Then winter came, with great snows. Crystalline nights. Air so cold it stung our nostrils. Moon, stars, and weak street lights reflected off the new snow, packed just right by a few motorists. We gathered out there at the top of the hill after supper, a bunch of us, not a car in sight. My brother and I wore Mackinaw coats, pilot caps with ear flaps down and tied under our chins, woolen mittens speckled with ice, black galoshes buckled tight over snow pants. Ready to fly.

With a hard running belly flop, we skimmed past our own house, past Ebsens' house, past Eleventh Avenue, past three other houses, past even the Krugers' house and on down almost to the Brewers' on English Boulevard, sometimes even dragging our feet to come to a stop.

A great run. It was a long climb back, but worth it. Clouds of steam poured out of our mouths as we slung our sleds under our arms, bent our heads against the incline, and trudged up through the snow to the starting point.

The sledding was so good that Stanley came out and took a few runs. Sometimes my brother and I performed our own version of the two-man luge: He lay on top of me and we rode a short distance to get up speed, then deliberately swerved to create a spill, tumbling off the sled and over each other, flopping as far as our momentum could take us.

One winter, inspired by the town's success in flooding a softball field to create an ice-skating rink, we decided to do the same at our house. We imagined the glossy surface of a small pond in our own backyard. Our father bought into our vision, or at least humored us in it. He helped us unroll the hose on frigid nights so we could spray water over a significant area. This was repeated on successive nights, but we awoke to nothing more than frost-covered grass. No ice skating here.

OUR PARENTS did not fuss about damage to the lawn. One summer we were allowed to create a miniature golf course. We dug nine holes, sinking used vegetable cans in each one. Two holes were in the front yard, one in the side yard, five in the back, with the final hole across the driveway on the same slope that had proved so difficult as a ski run.

The placement of the last hole was a mistake. Using our father's clubs, we tapped balls around the house, sinking them with great success. Then we came to the ninth hole. The approach shot needed to clear the driveway. If it didn't, the ball could easily skitter down the concrete, bounce into the street and take off for the bottom of the hill, just as our sleds did in winter. A badly hit ball resulted in a long chase.

Once past the driveway, we faced a serious obstacle in the sharp tilt of the land surrounding the last hole. Every missed shot rolled to the bottom of the slope. It took a near miracle to hole out and finish the round. We reduced the course to eight holes.

IT WAS easy enough to downsize football for four players on small lots, but backyard baseball was a problem. A real baseball or softball, hit with a real bat, sailed well beyond the boundaries of our small backyard. The ball might be lost forever, and chasing a ball into a cornfield or down a street took too much time away from the game. We had to find a way to miniaturize baseball.

We experimented with different types of balls and bats. Although we never played tennis, we had acquired some old tennis balls. We could throw a decent curve with a tennis ball, but when it was hit with a bat it went much too far. We tried using a broomstick instead of a bat, but it was almost impossible to hit the ball, and if we did get lucky, it still went too far, sailing over the hedge in the backyard and disappearing into a field.

When we came across a golf ball, we tried that, knowing full well it would be lost on the first solid hit. We also knew that a golf ball, driven back at the pitcher, could cause a knockout. We were glad to see them sail out of sight.

We tried marbles, which were hard to hit, but came off the bat like bullets. Safety concerns prevailed; we banned marbles.

Old socks bound up with tape were safe but lifeless. They landed softly in a fielder's hands, but did not fly far, or bounce at all.

Table tennis balls, light and hollow, curved wonderfully. With a little practice, we could master an arsenal of tricky pitches: a curve, a screwball, a drop ball, and a rising ball. We giggled with delight when we fooled a batter. If the ball was not hit solidly, it floated and danced in the air, giving a fielder time to get under it but also challenging him to track its wayward descent. The table tennis ball would have been perfect for two-person baseball games, but it had a fatal weakness: it broke easily. A solid hit cracked the ball, destroying its aerodynamics. There was nothing to do then but put a match to it and watch it sizzle into a small string of ash.

The perfect solution to backyard baseball did not appear until 1953. It was hollow and plastic, like the table tennis ball, but larger and tougher. It also had vents to facilitate throwing curves. It was called the Wiffle Ball, but it came too late for our games.

Backyard baseball never worked out. To play that sport we had to find larger fields and round up more boys.

## That Championship Summer

IN A town ringed by cornfields, with almost all houses on small lots, there were few open spaces for playing fields. The playground at Emerson School was by far the best and largest on the north side of town. It was a sports mecca for neighborhood boys, and often attracted boys who biked over from the south and west looking for action.

The school building and its grounds took up almost three square blocks, but the building was situated off-center, leaving the equivalent of several square blocks of open ground. It was an ideal football field, about half as big as the real thing, and we held games with as many as seven or eight players on a team. Sometimes high school players stopped by on Saturdays, bruised and hobbling a bit after their game the night before, but eager to play again.

The last Emerson School football game of the season was traditionally held on Thanksgiving afternoon, sometimes played on patches of ice and snow. Bill Lundquist, who lived across the street, christened this contest the Toilet Bowl.

When warm weather arrived, we turned to soft-ball. A diamond had been carved into the southwest corner of the playground by generations of boys who preceded us. The path from home to first was cut so deeply it could have been a dry streambed. The path to second base was shorter than the others, making the trip to third longer than it should have been, so that the diamond itself was off kilter. The pitcher's and batter's boxes were well eroded. The field itself was a hard mat of pebble-strewn earth with patches of exhausted grass. The top of a large boulder protruded out of the ground just behind and to the right-field side of second base.

There was no home plate or pitcher's rubber, no bags for bases. In casual play, we simply estimated the locations of these important markers. When the game was serious, we found pieces of cardboard or wood or clothing and used them for bases and home plate. Then we scratched an agreed-upon line in the dirt to mark the pitcher's rubber. This was to restrain the pitcher from inching closer to the plate and trying to overwhelm the hitter with fast ones.

There was no backstop behind home plate. Wild pitches and foul balls often rolled into Fourteenth Street, where the catcher had to chase them down, causing an exasperating interruption in the action. To prevent this, we arranged bicycles in a semi-circle behind the batter's box. This way, balls that squirted past the catcher bounced off the bikes' spokes and could be retrieved quickly. We used only the oldest bikes for this; a kid with a new one was excused from contributing.

The outfield was sharply asymmetrical, a Fenway Park in reverse. Right field was very short, while straight center and left swept away in distances that challenged the heaviest hitters. In right field, our equivalent of the "Green Monster"—Fenway Park's towering outfield wall—was the school building. Its brick wall with a bank of windows crowded into the outfield and appeared to be within easy reach of a left-handed power hitter. But the windows were protected in part by a large tree in short right-center field, and by the fact that left-handed power hitters were as rare as Eskimos. Our weakest glove man could patrol right field with no fear for the school windows.

A batter's best chance for a home run lay in center field. A hard-hit ball, even a grounder, that skirted left of the large tree and bounced past the center fielder could roll all the way up a small incline and hide under a set of teeter-totters near the school's back entrance. On a blow like that, a hitter could skip around the bases, hooting all the way as the center fielder trotted back in with the ball.

Left field was a hitter's dream. A stand of tall trees lined the far edge of the playground, almost a full block from home plate. The tree line was beyond the range of fifth graders, but when an older boy blasted one into their branches, we suspended play so he could trot around the bases like Babe Ruth.

The year I entered fifth grade at Emerson, my classmates and I, members of the oldest class in school and thus entitled to dominate the ballfield, began playing softball regularly during recess and lunch hours. We resumed our games that spring and eventually coalesced, with no involvement from the adult world whatsoever, into a sort of a team.

We continued to play often that summer, attracting boys from outside the neighborhood. Practices were held informally during the week, but we tried to hold a real game on Saturday afternoons.

Lineups changed constantly because players showed up—or didn't—according to their whims or obligations, and we could never be certain who would be diverted by chores or a trip to the dentist or an invitation to go fishing. I would not miss a game, and woke up on Saturday tingling with excitement. It's unlikely we ever assembled enough players to field two whole teams, so we plugged defensive vacancies with players from the batting team, and if anyone were watching, which they weren't, it would look as if a real game were in progress. Those of us who had balls, bats, and gloves brought them. Those who didn't used ours.

Kids showed up from other parts of town, and this is what probably led to a cross-town challenge. It was somehow determined that we fifth graders from Emerson would play the fifth graders from Lincoln School, which was located on the south side of town. This was a gutsy move on our part. Lincoln's fifth grade was larger than ours, and south side boys were, by reputation, tougher than we were. Never mind. We thrashed them. And just like that, we became fifth-grade softball champions of the whole town in a play-off of our own creation.

Typically we played without umpires. Perhaps for this game an interested parent or an older boy helped make calls at first base, but we did not call balls and strikes, leaving it to the hitter to choose his pitch. If a batter let too many good ones go by, we shouted ridicule at him until he began swinging. Stealing bases was not allowed. The outcomes of disputed plays were negotiated. For example, a questionable third-strike foul tick granted to an opponent in one inning could be redeemed in the next for a safe call on a contested force out.

Then came a shocking development: The Lincoln sixth grade wanted to play us. Somehow, our defeat of Lincoln's fifth grade had disgraced the sixth-graders, too, since both attended the same school. The older boys wanted revenge.

We knew that the challenge from the sixth grade was an invitation to disaster. For one thing, they had a larger pool of players. They were also older, bigger, stronger, faster, and meaner than we were. We decided to play them anyway.

Tom Domer remembered across the years that the Lincoln sixth-grade team included boys who would later be top athletes at Marion High School, including Shorty Novotny, Jerry Peck, and Harry Oakley— in other words, the best the sixth grade could throw at us. I remember only a hulking lineup of scowling strangers.

For this game, we would need umpires, if only to assure our personal safety, so we recruited my father to work first base. One or two other adults also officiated, including Mr. Kruger, a neighborhood dad, who was stationed near third base.

Our ace pitcher was John DeJong, who had perfected a low, accurate fastball through years of practice on a vacant lot next to his house. He also threw a spinning pitch that at least looked as if it were trying to curve. Tom Fisher was behind the plate, catching his neighbor's pitches just as he had in so many practice sessions.

Harold Hayes was at first base, a position for which he had unassailable credentials. He had been to Chicago, visited Wrigley Field, and observed the great Cub

first baseman, Phil Cavaretta, in action. The clinch-
er, however, was that Hayes owned a real first baseman's glove—an item of exquisite rarity in our circle.
Wally DeWoody, Tom Domer, Mike Kepros, and I were
somewhere in the field with two other boys. Based on
the single play I remember, I was probably shortstop
that day.

Spectators at our games were rare, but this one attracted a few. Some older boys lounged on their bikes.
A dog or two panted in the shade. An old man sat on
his camp stool. A few fathers stood quietly at a distance. Mothers would not consider showing up for this
sort of thing.

When the game started, I fully expected us to be
routed. But as the innings passed, we saw that we
had a chance. DeJong's fastball did not handcuff the
sixth-graders, but it did contain them, and we found
that we could hit and score against their pitchers.

We may have benefited from a more polished de-
fense. The only play I remember, and this one distinctly, was a popup by a sixth-grade hitter that curved foul
outside the third-base line. Our third baseman had to
back-pedal to his right, tracking the ball as it veered
into the branches of a tree and disappeared. Suddenly
the ball broke through the leaves and spun toward the
ground. Our third baseman snagged it.

It was a great catch and a big out. As the third baseman clutched the ball I gave a small cheer, which was
immediately cut off when Mr. Kruger called the batter
safe. Unfamiliar with the finer points of the rulebook,
he decided that the play did not count for an out because the ball was caught in foul territory.

The batter was allowed to stay at the plate. We
raised no howls of protest, nor did my father come

over from first base to try to undo the mistake. We accepted the call and played on.

FIFTY-SEVEN years later, at a class reunion, I saw Tom Fisher for the first time in half a century. One of the first questions I asked him was whether he remembered our great softball game that summer. He looked at me sharply and responded in a singsong voice, calling up a phrase we must have chanted that happy day:

*Nineteen to sixteen, the fifth grade beat the sixth grade!*

## *In Lyle's League*

HE COULD barely read and write.

He could not drive a car.

He had a severe speech impediment.

His mental abilities were about those of a twelve-year-old.

In the accepted language of his time, he was called retarded, although probably not to his face.

Against these disabilities, Lyle Touro was blessed with a generous heart, a sunny disposition, abiding optimism, a childish delight in being alive, and the perseverance of an ox.

He loved sports and he loved children, and out of these enthusiasms during his late twenties he decided to form a softball league for boys. Lyle dreamed big. He began his quest even before Little League was invented.

On weekends in the 1940s, Lyle Touro showed up at the town's playgrounds carrying a few bats, scuffed softballs, and rag-like fielders' gloves.

He asked the boys, Do you want to play in my league?

I was one who said yes. In those years, the idea of being in a league was thrilling and irresistible for a sports-mad sixth-grader whose entire athletic experience consisted of pick-up games. The year was about 1948, and I was turning twelve. My enthusiasm for Lyle's enterprise was obvious, and before long he recruited me to be one of his organizers. When he had settled on a time and place for practice, he called me on the telephone and instructed me to call four or five other boys with this information, then to report back to him.

It was hard to understand him at first, because he pronounced his *l* and *r* sounds like a *w*, so that his own name sounded like *Wy-oe Tu-woe*. He also slurred his words. He never lost patience with me, and in time I caught on. The incessant calls sometimes upset my mother, who otherwise seldom complained about her sons' manias. If I was away, she had to take the message. A telephone, she felt, was a device to be used sparingly. Lyle had exactly the opposite opinion.

In time, his players gathered at the town softball diamond, a stone-hard patch of clay near the football field. We were a motley assembly of boys in T-shirts, patched jeans, and canvas sneakers. Most of us played bareheaded because we did not own a baseball cap. I would have worn a Brooklyn Dodgers cap with pride, but team-branded apparel did not exist in our world.

For most town kids, the diamond was a mere bicycle ride away, but Lyle lived on his father's farm three or four miles out of town, and he couldn't drive a car. As practice time neared, he stopped work and, over his father's protests, headed for the road. Sometimes he pedaled his bicycle into town. Alternatively, he just started walking in that direction, counting on someone to drive by in a truck and give him a ride—which almost always happened.

Once assembled, Lyle's league seldom exceeded a dozen boys. Somehow, the low turnout never discouraged Lyle or his hard-core players. To us, it was still a league, or nearly one.

Lyle put us through a game-like training session in which we all played a variety of positions regardless of our skills. He stood outside the third-base line, shouting encouragement and instructions. He was stocky and heavy-set, clearly strong. He wore overalls, a cotton shirt, work boots, and a billed farmer's cap, which he sometimes tore off and threw in the dirt, exposing a shock of dry brown hair and his pale forehead, a sharp contrast to his suntanned face.

When he pitched his hat into the dust and stomped his feet he was not truly angry, just re-enacting some managerial behavior he had witnessed at a real ballpark. In some practices, players took turns serving as umpires, and if Lyle didn't like the call, he protested.

I pwo-test, he shouted. I pwo-test this game.

Lyle, we said, you can't protest. You run the league.

We understood, as Lyle may not have, that a manager's protest is a serious complaint that must be reviewed by league officials. If Lyle had to rule on his own protest, the complexities might bring the practice to a halt. But Lyle never took it that far.

I pwo-test anyway, he said, and we played on.

Some boys liked to tease Lyle about how seriously he took these games, but they seldom made cruel remarks about his disabilities. When a few tried it, others silenced them. Lyle was hard to tease because he tended to go along with jokes, enjoying them even if he wasn't sure what the point was.

I REMEMBER only one real game we played under Lyle's tutelage. Somehow, he had arranged a game against a team in Cedar Rapids. The game was memorable in at least two respects. For one, the outfield had real grass—a refinement that Marion's softball fields utterly lacked. For another, I made a sensational play, completely by accident.

I was stationed in left field when the batter smashed a hard line drive right at me. The ball came in a straight line and I could not tell whether it would drop in front of me, fly into my stomach, or soar over my head. So I stood there, watching it come, straight as a bullet.

Then I saw that the ball would go over my head. It had home run written all over it, and I would look like a fool for not tracking it down. The only face-saving option was to jump in the air and reach as high as I could with my gloved hand. That is what I did, and the ball hit my glove and stuck.

I was amazed to find the ball in the glove. I had turned what should have been a routine out into a circus catch. It was the third out, so I trotted to our bench, rolling the ball to the pitcher's mound.

When I got to the bench, Lyle was ecstatic. He was grinning and almost dancing with joy. I wish I had a Kodak of that, he said. I wish I had a Kodak of that.

So do I, Lyle, so do I.

## *The Boxing Club*

PERHAPS IT was the "Joe Palooka" comic strip in the *Cedar Rapids Gazette* that inspired me, at about the age of ten, to become a boxer. My dreams of glory in the ring distressed my father. Although he was a sports fan himself, he was wary of his son's interest in an activity that punished even the best in the business.

I had boxed once. On a rainy day at Camp Wapsie Y, the counselors matched willing boys of similar ages against one another in short bouts. There were four boys in my category. In the first match, a very strong boy—who looked as if he had experience—mercilessly pounded his opponent.

I drew an opponent as ignorant of the sport as I. He swarmed at me with flailing fists, and I closed my eyes, backed up, and stuck out my left hand. My attacker walked right into it. His nose caught the end of my glove, his eyes filled with tears, and he dropped his hands to his sides. I opened my eyes to witness the counselors stopping the fight. I had won on a TKO with a single punch. I was lucky and I knew it. Had I been matched against the stronger boy, I would have been seriously pummeled and probably discouraged from pursuing the sport.

Joe Palooka made it look easy. He was a blond heavyweight only slightly more intelligent than Li'l Abner, but his ring generalship was impeccable. He was a superb defensive fighter who packed dynamite in both fists. He also was a true American, dedicated to clean living, fair play, and good sportsmanship.

Joe did not fight often. The strip was devoted mostly to various predicaments involving Joe and his inner circle. The group included his manager and trainer, Knobby Walsh; Joe's girlfriend (and later wife), cheese heiress Ann Howe; and his enormous friend, Humphrey Pennyworth. But when Joe had a fight, I absorbed every move and even cut out the strips to make a scrapbook.

Boxing was a major professional sport in the 1940s, second only to baseball in popularity, with far more exposure than professional football or basketball. The *Gazette* ran boxing stories and photos almost daily, and there were national radio broadcasts from Madison Square Garden of major fights every Friday night.

There was a single champion in each weight division, and top contenders were, as Marlon Brando pointed out, "somebody." Joe Louis ruled the heavyweights, holding the crown through twenty-five fights over nearly twelve years, including a hiatus when he served in the army during World War II. He made personal appearances and fought exhibition matches, becoming an American hero.

Sugar Ray Robinson, "the greatest fighter pound for pound," not only then but perhaps for all time, won both the welterweight and middleweight titles. He was on the way to winning the light-heavyweight crown from Joey Maxim when he withered in the 103-degree heat under the lights at Yankee Stadium and was unable to answer the bell for the fourteenth round. Tony Zale and Rocky Graziano fought three epic battles at middleweight. Willie Pep, a featherweight, befuddled opponents with the slickest moves in boxing.

I studied magazines and books on the history of boxing. I learned about John L. Sullivan, who could lick any man in the house and catch a fly on the wing with his bare hand. Sunny Bob Fitzimmons was a broad-shouldered light heavyweight who brought down bigger men with his deadly solar-plexus punch. Jack Johnson, the great black champion, was persecuted because he defied white rule. Jack Dempsey weighed one hundred ninety pounds and fought with unbridled fury. I could recite from memory all the heavyweight champions, in order, from Sullivan to Louis.

I begged my father for boxing gloves. Before he gave in, Stanley made one last effort to dissuade me. He took me to a night at the Golden Gloves. These amateur tournaments were sponsored in Cedar Rapids by the *Gazette* and held in two rings set up in the Memorial Coliseum. I had never seen a real boxing match; my understanding of boxing came from reading and listening to the radio, neither of which delivered the full force of its cruelty.

My father hoped that the brutality of the Golden Gloves would open my eyes. For three rounds, mostly inept fighters unprotected by headgear flailed at one another to the point of exhaustion. I watched as tough farm boys and football players inflicted pain, drew blood, and delivered concussions. Instead of being repelled, I identified with the winners who most resembled Joe Palooka, took mental notes, and came away more committed than ever.

The set of gloves my father got me were beautiful. He did not skimp on his purchase; the two pairs were real leather with white laces, perhaps twelve or sixteen ounces, and definitely not toys. They were the only boxing gloves in our neighborhood. I began to introduce the manly art of self-defense to the boys of northeast Marion. We fought in front yards, backyards, side yards, vacant lots and, on cold or rainy days, in our basement.

Sometimes kids came from other parts of town to box. One guy I fought, a summer visitor, had a highly unorthodox style. He turned his left side toward his opponent with his glove up against his face, a one-armed peek-a-boo stance. His right arm, meanwhile, was extended full length behind him. This was his only weapon. When his opponent approached, he swung his right arm in a wide arc and banged his fist against his foe's body or head. He punched with one hand as if he were throwing a discus.

This style would have been duck soup for Joe Palooka or any classically trained fighter, such as I for instance. My plan was to dance in, throw a left jab to bring his guard down, and follow it with a right hook. Instead, as soon as I got close enough, my opponent launched his exaggerated bolo punch and I absorbed repeated hammer-like blows to my shoulders and ribs without scoring a clean hit. After the fight, I dismissed my defeat as meaningless, since the other guy didn't really know how to box.

I associate these events with memories of another summer visitor, a younger boy with a glass eye. He entertained us by using a grimy forefinger to slide the glass to one side so we could peer into his empty eye socket. It was pink and wet, and twitched. In deference to his condition, we did not allow him to box.

ONE DAY it came to me that we should form a boxing club. We would acquire a speed bag, a heavy bag, and other equipment and outfit my parents' small basement as a gym. I really wanted a speed bag. We could all train there, I thought. The funding mechanism would be a series of fights to be held in our basement. We would charge admission and the proceeds would go toward the equipment. I outlined my plan to my young friends, and they agreed to participate. Their enthusiasm for a boxing club seemed to equal mine.

We put together a card of about five fights. My father, concerned for the safety of the fighters, agreed to be referee. My mother muttered her disapproval several times but did not argue for a cancellation, at least not in my hearing.

As a special added attraction, I proposed to create a re-enactment of the heavyweight title fight between Joe Louis and Jersey Joe Wolcott. The fight was to be held a few weeks before ours, and restaging it, I thought, would have tremendous audience appeal, since Louis was widely expected to score an early knockout. The re-enactors would be two eight-year-old boys, my brother, Pete, and Bobby Kruger, from down the street.

We printed up flyers promoting our fight card and nailed them to telephone poles throughout the neighborhood. I can't remember the price of a ticket, but it was no more than a quarter; perhaps ten cents for children, twenty-five cents for adults.

A few weeks later, Wolcott stunned the fight world by going the full fifteen rounds against Louis. In the eyes of many, he won the fight, but Louis was awarded a split decision. Although I took notes on each round as it was broadcast blow-by-blow over the radio, we had no choice but to eliminate the re-enactment from the program as far too complex and insufficiently dramatic. We had the little kids fight each other in the opener.

On the day of the fight, we drew a standing-room-only crowd to the small basement of my parents' two-bedroom bungalow. We folded up the Ping Pong table in one corner to make room for about ten fans. Another ten or so sat on the wooden stairs, while a smaller number crowded in on either side of the stairs, though my mother's green wringer-washer took up a lot of space.

The boxing ring itself was a small open rectangle between the furnace and one wall. With ten boxers, one referee, and more than twenty spectators in her basement, my mother surely tried to retreat to the farthest corner of the house, but no matter where she went she was directly above the arena.

I had argued for three-round fights, like the Golden Gloves, but my father ruled that each bout would be only two two-minute rounds.

My opponent was Mike Kepros, whom I had never fought. I danced around on my toes, as I imagined Joe Palooka would, flicking out my left jab and looking for an opening. Kepros uncorked a round-house right that dumped me on the seat of my trunks. I bounced up immediately, unhurt, and we finished the contest without doing any damage. No one was keeping score, but had there been judges, they would have awarded the fight to Kepros. The knock-down was decisive.

The other fights were evenly matched and un-marked by injury. There were no other knockdowns.

After the fights, we counted our take. Several adults had generously contributed a dollar or more. Altogeth-er, the gate was less than ten dollars. I explained to my fellow club members that this would not be enough to equip our gym, but with additional fights and more fund-raising events, we could be certain of having a fine training facility.

That was when the fighters explained to me that they were not interested in having a club—especially since it would be in my basement and the equipment essentially my property. What they wanted, right now, was money, their share of the gate.

I realized that to resist would ruin my life. So we divided up the take, with perhaps a lesser share for the younger fighters.

Although we doubtlessly continued our impromp-tu fights for a time, and I remained a boxing fan for years, my career as a fighter lost momentum. I turned my energies to team sports.

I never got that speed bag, to the everlasting relief of my mother and father.

## *Jackie Robinson*

ON APRIL 15, 1947, a new hero burst on the American sports scene. Jackie Robinson was the first African-American to play Major League Baseball in modern times. As Robinson endured prejudice, then battled it, as he terrorized opposing pitchers with his hitting and base running, as he led his team to victories and then to pennants, he became the idol of a multitude of American boys of all races and religions.

I was one of them. Unlike most of the others, I later had the opportunity to tell Jackie Robinson in person what he meant to me.

It all started with a book.

In 1903, when Marion built its public library on Main Street with a gift of $10,000 from Andrew Carnegie, the architects placed cloakrooms on either side of the entrance foyer. The two long narrow rooms were intended, perhaps, to be used on one side by women and on the other by men. Some forty years later, when I discovered the library, the cloakrooms had been taken over by books. The alley-like room on the right, as you faced it, held books for young readers. There I discovered the Brooklyn Dodgers.

The Dodgers were the central team in a series of novels by John R. Tunis, a gifted writer of sports books for boys. The first Dodgers book was *The Kid from Tomkinsville*, then *The Kid Comes Back*, *Highpockets*, and others. I devoured them. At the age of ten or so I was only remotely aware of the real Dodgers, and had no conception of where Brooklyn was, but Tunis made me a fan. As I read his series, I transferred my love to the great "Boys of Summer"—Pee Wee Reese, Gil Hodges, Duke Snider, Carl Furillo, Roy Campanella, Preacher Roe, and especially Jackie Robinson.

Dodgers fans and Dodgers news were in short supply in Iowa. Fans there tended to root for the Cubs and Cards, whose games could be heard on the radio and whose fortunes dominated the scant space allocated to the major leagues by the *Cedar Rapids Gazette*. Box scores were my only consistent source of news about the Dodgers. I was a very lonely fan.

One summer afternoon, I idly twirled the dial of the small white radio in my bedroom. I heard the words, *Duke Snider is coming to the plate. He had a single in the first inning. . .* I was stunned. It was the Brooklyn Dodgers! In action! The voice was loud and clear. I held the radio in both hands, staring at the dial, memorizing the spot, terrified the voice would fade away and I would never find it again.

I had found the Dodgers, and I listened to their games every day, lying on my bed and staring at the radio. In time, I realized that the announcer was not in Brooklyn, but was receiving a description of the action by teletype and recreating the game on the air, and by some miracle it was being relayed to me. The announcer's moniker was Mason Dixon, and he spoke in a deep, resonant voice, as if history-making events were unfolding. In the background, a recording played the constant murmur of spectators, whose voices rose to a roar at exciting moments.

Dixon had a device that made a sharp crack when a batter connected. When a player hit a home run, he exclaimed, "There's a long drive, it could be . . . yes, TIMMM-BERRR!"

I don't remember that listeners were ever informed that Dixon wasn't actually at the park, but it soon became obvious. Generally, batters hit the ball, whether safely or for an out, on the first pitch. It usually took only three pitches to record a strikeout, and four for a walk. Consequently the game moved along briskly.

If the Dodgers were winning, I listened to every word, but if they were losing, I had to help. I got my old wooden bat, the thirty-six-incher, too heavy to use in real games, and went out to Eighteenth Street in front of our house. I threw rocks in the air and hit them downhill with my bat, crushing out singles, doubles, and homers for the Dodgers. Now I was Pee Wee, now Gil, now Jackie. The rocks tore holes in the bat, but it was worth it. Often, when I went back inside to pick up the action, the Dodgers had regained the lead.

It's hard to say, across all those years, exactly why I loved Jackie Robinson. He was a Dodger, and that was certainly part of it. I admired his extraordinary athleticism. I learned he had been the first person to letter in four sports at UCLA. One year as a football running back he averaged eleven yards per carry. He was an excellent basketball player. He was considered Olympic material as a broad jumper. In tennis, he won a national championship among black players.

Being only ten, and living in an all-white world untouched by television, I could not have well understood the brutal prejudice he was battling every day. But I knew enough to realize he was a martyr. During his first year in the majors, he was not allowed to retaliate when he was insulted, threatened, or injured. He had to turn the other cheek.

But he was a martyr triumphant. He played base-ball with an energy bordering on fury, beating his bit-terest foes at their own game. This made him a hero of mythic proportions.

Fan apparel licensed by the major leagues was unheard of in those days. Thus my life was bereft of Dodger memorabilia. Then it came to pass that I felt the need for a billfold, even though I had no money to put in a billfold, nor any photos to insert into the plastic sleeves. I must have aspired to ac-quire both. My mother, perhaps hoping to encour-age thrift, acquiesced. She knew I liked baseball, but she had scant knowledge of the details. She took the bus to Cedar Rapids and bought a zippered billfold of imitation leather that had a picture of Ted Williams on it. The portrait, printed in ink that had a tendency to flake off, showed Ted with a bat on his shoulders.

My mother did not know Ted Williams from Red Grange, so I showed as much gratitude as I could for the gift, even though I was not a fan of Williams, nor of his team, the Boston Red Sox, which was in the wrong league besides. Then my mother dropped a bombshell. She told me that the store also carried billfolds with pictures of two other players: Joe DiMaggio and Jackie Robinson.

She explained why she didn't buy the Jackie Rob-inson model. The salesman said you probably wouldn't want it because he's a Negro, she said. I tried to disguise my pain. Jackie's image would have been the greatest treasure my pocket could hold.

MANY YEARS later, when I was working in corporate public relations in New York City, I was able to meet my hero. It was in the late 1960s. Jackie Robinson, now deeply involved in civil rights, was to visit my boss, who ran our company's charitable foundation. I begged to be introduced.

When the day came, I stood in my office doorway and watched Jackie walk down the hallway in his distinctive, slightly pigeon-toed stride. He passed so closely I could have touched him. His hair had turned white, but he was big, about six feet tall and heavy in a powerful, muscular way.

Jackie did not glance in my direction. His eyes were on the one black secretary who worked with us, a quiet woman named Lillie Daniels. Jackie Robinson said hello to her. She barely looked up and softly said hello back to him.

I waited nervously until my boss called me to his office. I took a deep breath and went in. This is Jackie Robinson, my boss said. I can't remember shaking his hand, which probably means that I didn't. The power of Jackie's grip would have been unforgettable.

But I remember launching into the story of how I came to love the Dodgers, about hearing them play out in Iowa, about Mason Dixon and hitting rocks with my bat to help them win.

Jackie Robinson sat on the edge of my boss's sofa and stared at me. There was nothing pleasant in his expression. He was not exactly glowering, but his look made it clear that he didn't enjoy my story and had no intention of pretending to. He stared at me as if I were a noisy rookie who had interrupted a clubhouse discussion; a rookie who wasn't going to be around very long.

Under Robinson's stern gaze, my story ran down. He leaned forward on the very edge of the sofa, tensing as if ready to spring up. My boss tried to rescue the situation by saying something kind about my work. I looked to Robinson for approval. He offered none. He maintained his stony silence, looking me right in the eye without a glimmer of kindness.

He was enduring this moment with a fierce stoicism, I decided later, just as he had restrained himself during his first trying year in the majors.

I left the office in confusion. Soon Jackie Robinson came out. He said goodbye to Lillie Daniels, ignored me as I stood in my office doorway, took a right turn down the hallway, and walked out of my life forever.

Did the meeting change my feelings for Jackie Robinson? No. He was my hero forever. I was no more than an irksome moment, briefer than a gnat's buzz, in a great man's life.

# EPILOGUE:
## WHAT EVER HAPPENED TO. . .

# *What Happened to . . . .*

**Spike.** Our little dog suffered an ironic death. He liked to chase cars, but in this case he was running across the street to greet Pete when he was hit by a truck he did not see. He died instantly and Stanley and Pete buried him among some flowers in the backyard of our house on Seventeenth Street. I came home to the news and went to my room to cry.

**Emerson School.** At this writing Emerson School is still serving the youth of Marion. Children from pre-school through third grade attend the school, which was built in 1929. Many years ago the school was expanded with the addition of a large ell that consumed much of what was once the open playground. There is no room for softball. A six-foot-high fence encircles the school grounds, a safety precaution that also looks like an attempt to keep neighborhood kids from trespassing. I have driven by the school at least twenty times in the past decade and only once did I see any kids out on the grass—two girls who were just standing there.

I visited the school a few years ago and found that there were no longer any swings or teeter-totters, as they are considered too dangerous for small children. The railing from which our classmate fell was sealed off with impenetrable layers of wire fencing.

When I examined the patch of land that remained of our ball field, I found it covered with broad-bladed grass. There was no evidence of heavy use by anyone, no worn spots. During my visit, the school broke for lunch hour. The din from the gymnasium was deafening, but no kids came out to play, even though the weather was fine.

Plans to tear down the school were under consideration as this book went to press. No decision had been made about what to do with the land.

**Marion.** The town's population, about 5,000 in the 1940s, has swollen to more than 30,000. In the late 1980s, with some uptown buildings vacant and in serious disrepair, an entire square block was torn down— the block that had held the K-V Café, Harley Breed's barbershop, three beer taverns, the pool hall, the depot, and other enterprises. It was replaced by a strip mall.

Today, city leaders are attempting to preserve what remains of the uptown as an arts and entertainment center. The old Marion Theatre has gone through many incarnations in the past seventy years. For a time it showed X-rated films until outraged citizens shut it down. It burned down and was rebuilt. It became an office building. Today it has been turned into an intimate legitimate theater.

There is a plan in the works to install art in the alleys we patrolled as kids.

**Charlie's popcorn stand, the swimming pool, the root beer stand.** Gone.

**Cooper.** The school building disappeared decades ago. The population today is said to be about thirty, but "probably south of that," wrote journalist and resident Chuck Offenburger. Cooper had its moment of fame in 1981, its centennial year. To promote the anniversary, Cooper announced a search for its honorary fifty-first citizen, and who should volunteer but Iowan Johnny Carson, then host of the extremely popular *Tonight Show*. This led to an appearance on the show by some of the town's leading citizens and a centennial celebration that attracted more than twelve thousand people.

**Camp Wapsie Y.** According to a history of Central City, the lease on the camp expired in 1950. Three years later, a new camp was established upriver, near Coggon. The site features an ox-bow lake, perfect for boating, and a swimming pool to prevent muddy beards. The name was changed to YMCA Camp Wapsie. Pete served as a counselor there one year. The old camp's mess hall was moved to Prairieburg, Iowa, where it served as an addition to the Prairie Moon Ballroom until it burned down in 1995.

**Lyle Touro.** I wrote about Lyle Touro in my first book, which was really about Les Hipple. But I admired Tuoro so much and thought his story so worthwhile that I put it in the Hipple book. I should have saved it for this book, but I did not know at the time that there would be another book. A rookie mistake.

Lyle's smiling face after my Kodak-worthy catch is my last memory of him. Yet I must have seen him countless times afterward, for he sold his popping corn (shelled or by the ear) door-to-door, attended every sports event in town, and even took boys by bus to Cedar Rapids to see minor league baseball games.

Lyle never gave up his dream to form a league, and by 1957, a decade after I played for him, he had managed to assemble a three-team softball league. After each game, he dutifully went to the offices of the *Marion Sentinel* to report the result. Here is one game recap, in its entirety: "Touro's Tomcats defeated Rundquist's Yankees 13–4 Sunday at Emerson School. The same two teams meet again Aug. 11. Gary Larson was the winning pitcher for the Tomcats."

However, that very summer, Little League baseball came to Marion, effectively destroying Lyle's chances of keeping his league together. He continued for years to appear at summer playgrounds to organize softball games, but his major interest shifted to bowling. For decades he organized winter bowling leagues and tournaments for Marion boys. He solicited town merchants as sponsors, arranging for door prizes and trophies that Lyle, wearing a jacket and tie, presented at an annual supper at the Presbyterian Church. The supper was potluck, the food contributed by the boys' parents.

Not only did Lyle form and manage a bowling league in Marion, but he supported teams in other venues, too. One year in the late 1960s a Marion boy named Joe Petchulat joined a kids' league in Cedar Rapids. The team needed a sponsor and it found one: Touro's Popcorn. Joe remembered that Lyle attended some of the games to encourage his team. As he followed the action, Lyle jubilantly shouted "strike!" or "gutter ball!" celebrating triumph and failure as equals. His joy was so contagious, Joe wrote, "that we couldn't help but grin from ear to ear. He was a ton of fun."

The town honored him. To mark his retirement as a school crossing guard, the mayor declared "Lyle Touro Day," and he was presented with a plaque that read "Lyle Touro – Benefactor of Youth." When Lyle died at the age of seventy-eight in 1995, more than 150 people attended his funeral.

Speaking at his funeral, his nephew's wife, Linda Cory Touro, said, "I never heard him say a negative remark about any person, place, or thing. He never uttered a racial or sexist slur. He accepted and was serene. He believed in God without question or reservation. He perceived no person as his enemy. He treated all people as equals and with respect. He served his community. He gave unconditional love to family and friends and asked nothing in return."

Lyle Touro is a member of the Marion High School Athletic Hall of Fame.


**The sons of Stanley and Margaret.** Margaret and Stanley's sons graduated from Marion High School and went to college, then graduate school. Pete earned two master's degrees (in education from the University of Northern Iowa and in geology from Indiana University) and eventually headed the science department at St. Louis Community College. He later established the school's international education program, traveling widely and creating new programs, earning a reputation as a pioneer in the field among community colleges. He and his wife, Barbara, have three daughters. Pete and his family remained close to Margaret and Stanley, exchanging frequent visits with them.

I graduated from Cornell College, then earned a master's degree in journalism at Columbia University in New York. I had always wanted to go to New York. My ticket was an unusual fellowship at Columbia granted to Iowa-born students who went to college in Iowa. It was called the Lydia Roberts Fellowship, and it stipulated that the recipient must agree to return to Iowa for at least two years after the experience at Columbia. Clearly, Lydia Roberts cared for Iowa in a special way, believing that her fellowship would somehow enrich the state as its recipients returned home burnished by a few years of New York sophistication.

I had no taste for returning to Iowa, but I certainly didn't want to turn down the fellowship. I soon discovered that few Lydia Roberts fellows ever went back home. At Columbia, I was told that my only obligation was to write a letter saying I was *willing* to return to my home state, which I did, fibbing only a little. This betrayal of Lydia Roberts's grand intentions freed me to stay in a city that had called to me for years.

I married my Cornell College girlfriend while at Columbia. After receiving my master's in journalism, I was drafted by the army and stationed at West Point, where I worked in the information office, promoting the U.S. Military Academy and its cadets. When my tour ended, my wife and I traveled to Europe on five dollars a day. I worked briefly as an editor for Radio Free Europe in Munich, Germany. We returned to New York in 1962 and had a daughter and a son. We divorced about ten years later. During the anger and bitterness leading up to the divorce, and the hedonistic time for me that followed, I drifted away from my parents. In 1990, Elaine Goldman permitted me to become her husband. We had known each other for about ten years and loved each other for at least two. I continued to work in New York as a public relations executive and freelance writer and editor into my seventies.

**Stanley and Margaret.** Margaret, who could not remain still, was hired by the Marion school district to establish and manage what was called the "hot lunch program," which fed students at Lincoln School and the high school. Her previous work at Camp Wapsie Y had prepared her for this. She started the program in 1948, when I was in sixth grade. She worked at the school for many years, arriving early, leaving in mid-afternoon so she could be home in time to prepare supper for her family.

Stanley drove to Cedar Rapids each morning to his job at Allis Chalmers. He had an office job involving purchasing and quality control. In his last years on the job he hated it, perhaps because of personality conflicts. In summers, when Margaret was not working, he came home for lunch. Other times he packed his own, scrupulously avoiding calories. He ate a lot of celery, explaining to me that he had read that it takes more calories to chew a stalk of celery than can be absorbed from the amount swallowed. He wanted to remain as trim as possible. He was involved in civic activities in Marion and served as president of the Lions Club. He retained his interest in sports and for a time in the late 1950s and early 1960s was official scorekeeper at Marion High School home basketball games.

In 1950, the year I entered high school, the family moved to a larger house, about a block from the one they built. The move was made at least in part to provide a room for Margaret's mother, who suffered from Parkinson's disease.

Grandma Hartung's personality consisted of a deep stoicism that seemed to border on anger. I saw nothing lovable about her. She wore a plastic bib when she ate because food dribbled from her fork or spoon, trickling down her chin to the bib, which I found repulsive.

During the day she watched television, sitting close to the set in an upholstered chair. Sometimes Pete and I joined her as she watched the Arthur Godfrey or Ed Sullivan shows. She did not react to the entertainment at all; she just watched silently. Occasionally she asked Pete or me whether one of the performers was a Negro. The TV reception, in black and white, was blurry and perhaps her eyesight was as well. Sometimes Pete or I answered truthfully and sometimes we lied about it, stifling our giggles. It didn't matter. Grandma Hartung noted the information and made no further comment.

Margaret always said that when the time came she would go willingly to a nursing home. The experience of tending to her mother strengthened her resolve in this matter.

After their children left home, Margaret and Stanley began to eat out more often. They joined the "club" at the Flame Room in Cedar Rapids, where their membership permitted them to take liquor by the drink, still generally forbidden in Iowa. For many years after that, they enjoyed a nightly martini or two, which Stanley mixed promptly at 5:00 p.m. and served with crushed ice in dainty little green juice glasses.

Sometime in the 1960s, Stanley received an offer for early retirement, and he and Margaret moved to Lakeview, Arkansas, near Bull Shoals Lake, a huge reservoir created in 1952. The area was drawing retirees from the north who sought warmer winters and economical living in the Ozarks. They bought a small house with a screened back porch looking out over a nice-sized backyard that attracted hummingbirds.

Stanley bought a rowboat with an outboard motor and spent many days fishing quietly on Bull Shoals Lake.

Margaret found work in a local gift shop, where she earned very little money but was kept busy chatting with the trickle of tourists who visited the store. She also got to know some hillbilly woodcarvers whose work was attracting attention.

The star carver was a young man named Junior Cobb, who could neither read nor write, and who came out of the hollows with new carvings only when he needed money. In time, Cobb and his work became widely known. He supported a wife and five children solely by his art (and by what he could gather in the woods). It has been written that Junior Cobb visited the White House and carved his initials in Jimmy Carter's desk and that his work has been preserved by the Smithsonian Institution. Margaret bought some of Junior Cobb's finest small works. I'm looking now at an eight-inch carving of a man in overalls, his head tilted back as he gulps a fiery drink of moonshine from a jug.

At home, Stanley watched the Cubs play on TV, the sound turned off because his hearing was going bad. He had no trouble following the action without advice from the announcers. Margaret sat nearby, crocheting afghans. Throughout her later life she made scores of these shawls, maybe hundreds, selling them at cost, giving them away, pulling them apart after they were made and then remaking them. Her hands had to be busy.

They lived frugally, saving a portion of their retirement income, continuing to build a nest egg. Eventually they sold the house in Lakeview and moved to a small apartment in nearby Mountain Home. "I finally bought a washer and dryer, I'm not sure I like them," Margaret wrote. Up until then she had always used a tub washer with an attached wringer. "I guess the only thing I miss living in an apartment is a clothes line."

As Stanley entered his eighties, his health declined and he eventually entered the hospital in a hospice situation. Pete and his family continued to make regular visits from St. Louis. Elaine and I, recently married, flew to St. Louis and drove to Arkansas with Pete and his wife, Barbara. Stanley had asked us not to make the trip. Elaine and I had visited previously; Stanley did not want us to see him in such bad condition.

When we arrived at his hospital room, he had just awoken from a nap and was in the grip of a dream about visiting Pittsburgh. He told us about the dream in a cheerful, jazzy way I had never heard him talk. I imagined he was inspired by pain-killing drugs. He made us laugh with his visions of a city he had never visited. Margaret went to his bedside. They had a brief conversation we couldn't hear, then they kissed, a solid, meaningful kiss. It surprised and slightly embarrassed me. I was not sure I had ever seen them kiss before.

After a while, I was left alone in the room with my father. I did not know what to say. I had written him several letters telling him how grateful I was for all he had done for me. I told him that I knew he loved me and I now realized how much that love had sustained me, had given me a sense of security all my life, a love I continued to draw upon every day.

I may have said in those letters the words I love you, but I probably did not. I have no memory of either of my parents saying they loved me, but I never doubted that they did. In any event the words did not come out of my lips as I stood near my father's bed. He closed his eyes and we sat together for perhaps ten minutes without speaking. I thought he might be asleep. I got up to leave. He opened his eyes and looked at me. I went to him, put my right hand on the back of his head and looked into his eyes. I could not say anything. Then I left the room.

Stanley died a few weeks later, in January 1991, three months before his eighty-fourth birthday. He wanted no funeral or ceremony of any kind. His body was cremated. During this time, Margaret shed no tears. Pete, who broke down several times, asked her why she didn't cry. I've done my crying already, she said.

In March, I flew to St. Louis and rode with Pete to Cedar Rapids, where we delivered Stanley's ashes to the mausoleum at Cedar Memorial Park. I asked Pete to open the case that held our father's ashes. We stood at the back of his SUV and examined the contents of the case: gray, powdery sand. I thought there should be more of him there.

The day was cold and overcast with heavy clouds low in the sky. A bitter March day any Iowan would recognize. The sky was spitting a few bits of snow or ice into a brisk wind, and we ducked our heads slightly to keep from being stung by the flakes. Inside the mausoleum, an attendant opened the door to a small vault in the wall that Margaret and Stanley had purchased many years earlier. Pete placed the case in its slot and the attendant closed it up. The attendant asked us if we wanted to pause for a moment, to reflect or pray. Pete said no. Then Pete and I went out for a drink.

Margaret moved from Arkansas to an independent living facility not far from Pete's house. She had a small apartment and took most of her meals in the dining room. Pete visited her almost every day and was always on call for errands. Margaret had little desire to go out. Her shopping requests were specific and she insisted on reviewing the receipts. She wanted to know what things cost. She refused to reimburse Pete if he picked the wrong item or bought more than she had ordered. When Margaret asked Pete to get her a banana she wanted one banana. She specified white Dial soap, a single bar, even though the bars usually came in multipacks. Pete had to break open the pack and carry the extras in his car.

Margaret took exception to the grammatical errors committed by her fellow residents. She made a list of them and reported them to Pete. She hated double negatives. She and Stanley had been avid bridge players for decades, and when Margaret joined card games at the retirement home, she won so frequently that the other residents refused to play with her. She called the residents "inmates," and when that usage was challenged, she was ready with a dictionary definition: "any of a group occupying a single place of residence."

I visited a few times. For several years when my birthdays came around I marked the occasion by writing Margaret a letter thanking her for all she had done for me.

At the age of ninety, Margaret decided to cut her cigarette consumption to a pack a day. A few years later her health grew worse and she entered a nursing home, sharing a room. Smoking became a hassle and she quit.

Margaret had trouble sleeping at night, and roamed through the nursing home's halls, which were built in a circle. It was as if she were doing laps. In the morning, attendants often found her sleeping in a hallway chair. She was tormented by a scalp itch that no salve or rinse could cure. She bore all this stoically.

One day a nurse called Pete and told him Margaret was dying. Although she was medicated for pain, Margaret recognized her son and daughter-in-law. She wore a pair of slippers and she asked Barbara to look in her closet to see how many pairs of shoes were there. Barbara looked and told Margaret there were two pairs.

Margaret asked, So I have three pairs? Then I can die now?

Yes, you may, her son answered.

That was March 5, 2000. Margaret was ninety-three.

A few days later, Pete and I took her ashes to Cedar Memorial. The weather was exactly the same as it had been when we delivered Stanley's ashes: low cloud-darkened skies and a cold wind driving sharp bits of snow. Pete put Margaret's remains next to Stanley's. This was done without words or ceremony, just as we had done with Stanley's ashes nine years earlier.

I have made many trips to Marion since that time. Sometimes I go to the mausoleum. A chair is near the vault that holds the ashes of my parents. I sit there for a while, look at my parents' names on the vault, and try to empty my mind of everything but gratitude.

## *Acknowledgements*

I am extremely grateful to Kari Johnston, who designed this book and helped me navigate the uncertain waters of self-publishing to see it into print. I especially thank Ben Miller, Anne Pierson Wiese, Pete Kellams, Shirley Pantini, and Joyce Hutchins for reading drafts of the book and offering comments. Thanks to Holly Chapman for her sharp editor's eye. Thanks to artist Karen Hoyt and the Marion Heritage Center for allowing parts of the Main Street mosaic to appear on the book's cover. As well as those mentioned, I thank the following for contributing their memories and providing help in other ways: Garth Baker, John Ballard, Phyllis Carlson Davis, John DeJong, Wally DeWoody, Tom Domer, Tom Fisher, Mollie Keith Foti, Harold Hutchins, Jay Kacena, Chuck Kent, Bill Lundquist, Dick Mohr, Elaine McGee O'Malley, Tony Pantini, Mary Lou Pazour, Joe Petchulat, Ed Reed, Steve Roth, Shirley Shireman, Harvey Sollberger, Keith Smith, Dick Todd, Ken and Linda Tuoro, John Vernon, Jerry Walker. And, to Elaine, thank you for everything.

# Praise For Dan Kellams's

## *A Coach's Life: Les Hipple and the Marion Indians*

"A poignant biography of the stern taskmaster . . . the historical background of the town grips the reader."
— Jim Ecker, *Metro Sports Report.*

"Compelling . . . An empathetic recollection of a man and a time that no longer exist. . . A story both to enjoy and contemplate."
— Foreword Clarion Reviews.

"Not just a book about a man and his accomplishments . . . a thoughtful piece of small-town history."
— Paul Ingram, Prairie Lights bookstore.

"You see the rules, meet the athletes and coaches, read the stories of championship seasons, learn of the coach's demise in the midst of school politics and parental outcries."
— Dave Rasdal, *Cedar Rapids Gazette.*

"Part *Hoosiers* and part *Our Town* . . . Marion, Iowa, becomes Hickory, Indiana, or Grover's Corners, New Hampshire . . . Kellams treats Hipple as Hipple probably treated him. Tough and to the point."
— Phil Grose, author of *South Carolina on the Brink.*

"Mesmerizing . . . Kellams weaves a really good yarn."
— Judy Fremont, president, WVOX radio.

"A fantastic book!"
— Scott Unash, KGYM radio.

"[Marion athletes] were called 'Hipplemen,' and they still talk in reverent tones about the coach who shaped their lives."
— *Iowa History Journal.*

**Available from all online book retailers.**